Ten Common Myths
in
American Education

Mordechai Gordon

TEN COMMON MYTHS IN AMERICAN EDUCATION
ISBN: 1-885580-18-5

COPYRIGHT 2005 BY HOLISTIC EDUCATION PRESS,
P.O. BOX 328, BRANDON, VT 05733-0328
WWW.GREAT-IDEAS.ORG
1-800-639-4122

Dedication

To my first teachers, my parents,

Rachela and Haim Gordon

And to my students,

who continuously inspire me

with thoughtful and challenging questions.

Acknowledgments

I would like to thank Charles Jakiela, my editor and publisher at Holistic Education Press, who had faith in this project and provided me with great support and invaluable insights throughout this project. I would like to acknowledge my colleague and friend, Kevin Basmadjian, for his feedback and help in editing major parts of this book. Special thanks are also due to Hans Bergmann, Dean of the College of Liberal Arts at Quinnipiac University, for the financial support he provided that enabled me to complete this book on time. I am grateful to Joe Kincheloe, great scholar and friend, who gave me a lot of encouragement and wrote the Foreword to the book. Finally, I would like to thank my wife, Gabriela, for her patience, understanding, and support during my work on this project.

Table of Contents

Ten Common Myths in American Education

Mordechai Gordon

Foreword

Joe L. Kincheloe

It is my pleasure to write an introduction to *Ten Common Myths in American Education*. Mordechai Gordon has emerged in just the last few years as one of the top educational foundations scholars in North America. His ability to get to the heart of an issue, to make educational and moral meaning in ambiguous situations, and to express his ideas in a clear, concise, and compelling manner is treasured by those of us interested in the social, cultural, and philosophical contexts in which education takes place. Because of the clarity and accessibility of his work, I believe that Gordon's talent will be appreciated by wider and wider audiences in the coming years. In this context, *Ten Common Myths* presents Mordechai Gordon at the top of his game. Educational leaders, education students, and teachers need to read this book — especially at this ominous juncture in the history of education.

Gordon is distressed by contemporary ideological efforts to standardize, test, and control what occurs in American classrooms. As he delineates these ten mistaken beliefs, Gordon points out the reductionism, the faulty reasoning behind these twenty-first century educational reforms. In particular, he analyzes the type of thinking that leads to such misconceptions and, in turn, to misguided and damaging educational policies. These simpleminded solutions, Gordon asserts, fail to comprehend (or don't want to comprehend) the complex realities that have led to particular educational problems. When right-wing scholars make assertions — such as the argument that teacher education does not improve teaching — they are engaged not only in faulty reasoning but also in blatant duplicity. Gordon takes on these ideologues, presenting a critique and alternatives to such widely distributed work. Understanding what is at stake, he carefully informs his readers that the survival of public education swings in the balance. Those interested in the future of education and schooling would be well served to carefully consider the author's ideas in this context.

Framed in this disturbing context, *Ten Common Myths in American Education* deftly deals with questions of educational purpose. Gordon, the philosopher of education, offers compelling insights into one of his favorite topics: We must get beyond a nuts-and-bolts mentality, he warns us, that substitutes methods and techniques for profound inquiries into what teachers in a democratic schools should work to accomplish. When we think about the moral, cognitive, affective, political, and social dimensions of what constitutes an educated person, we begin to realize the complexity of the pedagogical task. In this context we begin to understand the intricate relationship between the social context in which education takes place, the needs of society, the needs of individuals, and how all of these dynamics must be accounted for in the contemplation of purpose. Methods and techniques are empty mechanisms when studied outside of these insights. They must always be connected to larger intellectual, social, political, and moral purposes. This is what Gordon helps us do in this book. As he points out common misconceptions, he clarifies our efforts to figure out what education is all about and to discern the goals that motivate our actions.

With the question of purpose permeating every chapter of the book, Gordon courageously moves into the political domain. As he examines multicultural education in relation to the structure of society, the author moves into the domain of power and its distribution. By bringing power and social structures into the mix, Gordon transcends facile and misleading discussions of cultural issues in education. At the same time, he provides us with typically erased insights into purpose — in particular, how dominant power operates to shape the goals of schooling. Indeed, Gordon points out, power wielders shape the purpose of school in a way that is fundamentally unfair to those students who come from poor or non-white backgrounds. In this context, he asks readers to consider what we might do about an educational system that operates within and as a functioning part of inequitable social structures? Here, Gordon engages readers in an analysis of the ways that schools attempt to adapt students to such an unfair system. Is it our moral duty to change such a system? Is one dimension of school purpose in a democratic society related to providing special help to those who are victimized by such a system?

In this context, Gordon raises the topic of critical pedagogy — a tradition close to my identity as a scholar and teacher. In a critical pedagogical classroom students gain a literacy of power and its effects. In situations informed by critical pedagogy teachers develop an understanding of how power asymmetries shape not only school goals but their own consciousness of what it means to be a teacher. Is the teacher an agent of the dominant culture and the oppressive status quo who works to justify the actions of dominant power in his or her classroom? Or is the teacher a moral agent who frames the curriculum in terms of the promises of democracy and society's failures to live up to those promises? Gordon expertly answers such questions as he promotes what I have described elsewhere as "a view from low places." What Gordon and I mean by such a concept involves the importance of gaining new perspectives on such questions from exactly those individuals who have never been asked their opinion — those men and women with the least power.

Gordon stretches the pedagogical and moral imagination of his readers, contending that we can make schools more free, equal, and just only when we seriously listen to the voices of the marginalized. Many readers, of course, will never have encountered such moral and political discourses in their formal schooling or even in their everyday lives. Because of such a lack of exposure they may find Gordon's discussion shocking or somehow out of place in a book on education. Such a reaction in a society that claims to be democratic and egalitarian moves us to realize just how important Gordon's work really is. Indeed, such a response tells us that we live in a time of a truncated public understanding of democracy. The author's embrace of such issues is central to his effort to clear up these damaging myths about the educational sphere. Please pay close attention to Gordon's words in this domain; they have the kinetic power to change lives. And from my perspective lives need to be changed in this era, an epoch that is not especially friendly to the practice of democracy and democratic schooling.

Introduction

"We live in fictitious times," to borrow a phrase from Michael Moore's 2003 Oscars acceptance speech. We live at a time in which the distinction between reality and fiction in the United States is becoming increasingly blurred not only in politics but also in education. We are bombarded in the media with reports about testing, standards, and accountability as well as the quality of today's schools and teachers — without being given a clear sense of the significance of the issues that are under debate. We are being told that many students are not performing up to par, that too many teachers are not qualified to teach, and that schools are not holding teachers and students accountable for achieving high standards. Yet amidst all the rhetoric about the failure of many public schools and the problems with the education system in general, there is much confusion and lack of clarity about the meaning of basic educational issues such as teaching and learning, testing and accountability, and standards and the curriculum. Similarly, the educational policy initiatives of the No Child Left Behind Act rest on some serious misconceptions about the main issues that are at stake (See Elmore 2002 and Lewis 2002).

How do I know that there are so many misconceptions and myths being disseminated about education? To begin with, as a teacher educator, I have taught and researched many of the core and contentious topics in this field, topics such as classroom management, the meaning of the "Basics" in education, integrating technology into schools, accountability and testing, and multicultural education. More importantly, I have listened carefully to my students' questions and paid close attention to their misconceptions for over a decade. This experience has convinced me that the mistaken beliefs shared by many teacher candidates — and educators in general — thwart their attempts to gain a clear understanding of some of the most important issues in education. If we do not help our students question their beliefs and ideas about education, their misconceptions can ultimately undermine their efforts to become good teachers.

For this reason I chose to write *Ten Common Myths in American Education*, a book aimed at addressing the most prevalent questions and misconceptions of teacher candidates and educators in general. Although this book is philosophically grounded and research based, I have made every effort to explain the issues and the misconceptions surrounding them in a clear and accessible manner so that everyone could understand them. To this end, the discussions in this book include many examples from my own experiences and from those of other teachers that illustrate the arguments that I am making. In addition, the book integrates many stories and anecdotes into the discussion, some of them my own while others are borrowed from different literary and educational texts. However, in putting so much emphasis on clarity and accessibility, it is not my intention to oversimplify educational issues and problems that are certainly complex and multifaceted. It is rather to encourage teacher candidates and other educators to think more systematically and critically about the issues that affect them. The references at the end of the book direct readers to some of the most important and comprehensive sources on the topic.

The research that this book is based on is primarily interpretative as opposed to empirical, though there are a number of references made to empirical studies conducted by other scholars. That is, my research is not based first and foremost on systematic observations conducted in classrooms, surveys administered to principals, or interviews with teachers. Rather, the method of analysis employed here relies heavily on *synthesizing* various studies that have been done by other researchers on the relevant topic and then *interpreting* the results of these studies in a way that supports my own argument. In effect, I borrow insights from other educators and scholars that can help me shed light on the ten myths I have identified as well as on how to address the issues with greater depth and clarity.

Yet what makes this method of analysis a legitimate way of doing research in education? First, it should be pointed out that most scholars recognize that there is more than one way of conducting rigorous scientific research in the field of education and that both quantitative and qualitative studies are legitimate. Whereas the former refer to ways of conducting research that concentrate on those variables that lend themselves to numerical expression, the latter points to approaches that focus on the *meanings* that human beings give to their actions and attitudes. In recent years qualitative research, which includes interpretation as one of its methods, has gained greater popularity and credibility not only in education but also throughout the social sciences. The rise of qualitative research in education came about in large part due to the recognition that in this realm we are dealing with human subjects who are meaning makers and are actively involved in the process of interpreting the world and their relationship to it.

Thus in basing my research on synthesis and interpretation rather than on numerical data and statistical analysis, I wholly embrace the conviction of qualitative researchers that human and educational events are better understood than counted. Still, someone might wonder what makes my study unique or original since the ten topics that are addressed in this book are not really new and have previously been discussed is some depth. This is a legitimate question, though it presupposes a traditional notion of originality, one to which I do not subscribe. Traditionally, being original meant that a person had to discover that single element, make that unique argument, or find that one law or theory that had never existed beforehand. I reject this definition of being original not because it is incorrect but because it is too narrow and limiting. Human beings live and operate in a social context that includes family, friends, community, and many other groups of people. They constantly get ideas from other people, books, the media, and a host of other sources with whom they interact. As such, it is virtually impossible, especially with the amount of information that is at our disposal today, that someone will discover something that is entirely new or unprecedented.

However, the fact that each one of us is influenced by other people, texts, and ideas, and that it is extremely difficult to articulate something completely unique, does not mean that we can no longer be original. Instead, this fact indicates that we must *reformulate* what it means to be original in order to broaden the traditional definition so that we take into account the influence of the social context. Once we acknowledge the impact of society on us, we realize that being original can mean taking an idea that was invented in one context and applying it to another set of conditions and circumstances. Likewise, being original can mean appropriating a concept that was invented by someone else and using it to analyze and evaluate a new problem. From this perspective, being original can also refer to the ability to synthesize ideas from different sources and integrate them to construct a unique argument. These are only a few of the many ways of being original that take into account the impact of the social context on people. What unites most, if not all, of these ways is a shift in perspective and the ability to look at an issue or problem in a different and more complex manner.

Each chapter in this book takes on an important topic and analyzes it from a perspective not usually heard in discussions and debates on education. Equally significant is the fact that the examination of these topics takes place in the context of some of the most common misconceptions in education, a context that has not received much attention so far. In short, it is the perspective and the context rather than the topics themselves that are new here. Although there are a number of references made in later chapters to earlier ones, each chapter is meant to stand on its own. Thus the readers are welcome to read the book in order or skip individual chapters to get to the ones that most interest them.

In Chapter One, "Good Teaching Means Following a Recipe," I take on the widespread myth that good teaching entails acquiring a bag of tricks or a number of proven techniques that can then be applied to the classroom. I call this approach the "teaching-as-recipe model" and argue that it is not adequate for the problems and issues that teachers face every day. Instead, I propose the "teaching-as-challenge model," an approach that emphasizes the intellectual and scholarly nature of this profession. This latter model asserts that good teaching should not be viewed as a technical act but rather as an art or a craft that constantly involves challenging oneself with new goals and ideas. I conclude this chapter by identifying some of the main challenges that teachers face in their work with students.

The second chapter, "Theories Can Be Applied Directly to Practice" addresses perhaps the number one question that teacher candidates raise in their education courses. It deals with the relevance of theory to practice and with the view, shared by many teachers, that the theories they learn have nothing to do with the issues and problems that come up in the classroom. I suggest that one of the main reasons for the mismatch between theory and practice is related to a misleading notion of applied theory and to a failure to appreciate theories as social-historical constructs. In my view, an educational theory cannot just be taken in its entirety and put into practice in any given classroom. In the final part of this chapter, I propose four alternative ways of applying educational insights to one's teaching.

The next chapter, "Students Need to Know 'The Basics' " deals with the problematic way in which the Basics have been generally viewed —

as a set of essential facts that need to be memorized. Instead of viewing the mastery of these facts as merely a means of attaining some higher educational purpose such as critical thinking or creativity, the acquisition of information itself has been elevated to the level of one of the most important educational goals. I argue that memorizing the basic concepts, formulas, or events of a particular discipline makes no sense unless one can use this information to gain a deeper understanding of the subject. Such an understanding assumes that a person has grasped the significance of the facts and their relationship to other data, and can determine in what contexts they can be applied. The final part of this chapter provides the reader with some valuable suggestions and illustrations on teaching the Basics.

Chapter Four, "Keeping Students Busy Enhances Learning," focuses on a number of practices instituted in many schools to keep students busy. Contrary to popular belief, I suggest that practices such as "do-nows," reduced recess, and increased time on-task have very limited educational value and are used primarily to control students. I also analyze a number of equally problematic assumptions about the nature of children, knowledge, and the social context that are at the basis of many classroom management models. These assumptions lead many teachers and schools to prize silence over excitement, obedience over critical thinking, and rote learning over creativity. Beginning with an alternative set of postulates, I argue that teachers need to promote rather than discourage opportunities for interaction, dialogue, and collaboration among students. From this perspective, schools will need to refocus their energies on engaging students in meaningful activities rather than on managing and controlling their behavior.

The next chapter, "Confusion and Uncertainty Hinder Learning" addresses the widespread view that confusion hurts students and that teachers should always make their expectations and objectives crystal clear to their students. I show that this belief is based on the misguided notion that performance on standardized tests is the same as genuine learning and understanding. In addition, the view that confusion hurts students is informed by a fallacious notion that human existence is a clear, straightforward, and unequivocal reality. Rather, the world in which we live in and interact with other people is full of confusions, ambiguities, and shades of gray. Creating a space for perplexity and uncertainty in our classrooms is therefore crucial to fostering citizens who are critical and independent thinkers. I conclude this chapter by proposing a number of ways in which teachers can help students welcome confusion and embrace uncertainty.

The topic of technology and our infatuation with it is the focus of the next chapter. In "Technology is the Cure for All Problems in Education," I examine the common view that integrating technology into the lesson will always lead to better learning and show that it is based on various myths and falsehoods about its value. The beliefs that the mere availability of technology in schools would result in its extensive use, that the increased availability and use of this technology would lead to higher student achievement, and that integration of technology into schools would produce students who are more educated are all misleading. My analysis suggests that teachers, administrators, policymakers, and educators in general need to become more aware of the advantages and limitations of computer and information technologies and more sensible about the push to integrate these machines into classrooms.

Chapter Seven, "Good Techniques are Those that Seem to 'Work'," addresses the scarcity of ethical discourse in education and the problem of focusing on what "works." By celebrating what works, many teacher candidates and new teachers are disregarding the important issue of educational purpose as well as the distinction between two levels of analysis: the actual and the desirable. This means that techniques, strategies, and rules that work are often automatically assumed to be good without any serious moral reflection. Yet addressing ethical issues is vital since most educational decisions and practices have serious moral consequences and many teachers and administrators are not really conscious of the moral implications of their actions. I argue that holistic thinking is an approach to education that can help us overcome the limitations of conventional educational discourse because it emphasizes questions of purpose, meaning, and ethics.

The next chapter, "More Testing Results in Higher Standards," critically interrogates two misconceptions that are at the basis of our current fascination with standards-based reforms. First is the widespread notion that the achievement of high or rigorous standards consists of the acquisition of a set of prescribed ideas, formulas, and skills. However, my research suggests that this conception of high standards is very narrow and technical, puts a premium on quantity over quality, and undermines the most important function of schooling. Equally troubling is the false notion that the best way to assess the attainment of high standards is by requiring students to demonstrate their performance on standardized exams. In fact, the vast majority of high-stakes tests do not accurately assess how well teachers are instructing their students and that these testing instruments actually do more harm than good to children. I close this chapter by discussing an alternative way of conceptualizing student and teacher assessment, an approach that is aimed solely at enhancing teaching and learning.

Chapter Nine, "Multicultural Education: It's Only About Heroes and Holidays," addresses the hot topic of multicultural education and the common misconception that it is essentially about the acknowledgment of the heroes, holidays, and traditions of different cultures. Indeed, many teachers and schools wrongly interpret multiculturalism in a narrow, bland, and politically correct way so as not to offend anybody. They therefore miss the essence of multicultural education, which is aimed at raising students' awareness of various forms of discrimination, injustice, and racism that occurred in the past and still exist today. In addition, multicultural education should not be equated with mere content integration or limited to a particular class period that is taught by a specialist, as is done in many schools. Rather, it must be viewed as a comprehensive approach that is integrated throughout the school culture and receives the same weight as other core subjects.

Finally, the last chapter, "Easy Solutions Work in Education," considers the wisdom of two federal policy initiatives: No Child Left Behind and federal proposal to deregulate teacher education. My research suggests that these federal policies rest on the misguided beliefs of a number of educational leaders who seem to be more interested in finding quick fixes to complex educational problems than in understanding their underlying causes. Moreover, the accountability component of the No Child Left Behind Act and initiatives to deregulate teacher education are neither supported by scientifically based research nor grounded in the collective experiences of excellent teachers. In order to address the achievement gap between white, middle-class, and minority lower-class students as well as the shortage of qualified teachers, educators will have to avoid the temptation of seizing on to quick and easy fixes to complex problems. They will need to reclaim the Socratic legacy of critical thinking: a continuous process of questioning, doubting, and evaluating one's beliefs and conclusions that does not end until one gets to the underlying causes of the problem.

The ten chapters in this book are written primarily for teacher candidates, teacher educators, and new teachers. My hope is that these essays

will address some of the most common perplexities, questions, and misconceptions that teachers and educators in general have about their vocation. At the very least, I would hope that this book would help readers
view the profession of teaching in a different context and from a fresh
perspective, one that is much more complex and critical than is offered
by conventional discourses on education. As Socrates reminds us in the
dialogues of Plato, such a perspective is crucial not only to better understand what we are doing but also to bring about meaningful changes in
education.

Chapter One

Good Teaching Means Following a Recipe

During my tenure as a teacher educator, I have often noticed that many students come to us looking for recipes, for a bag of tricks that they can take with them and apply in their classrooms. They assume that if they could just acquire these techniques and skills they will be good teachers or at least survive in the urban public schools. While I am not against teaching students worthy techniques in classroom management, for instance, I seriously doubt that knowing these techniques will make them good teachers or even allow them to survive in many of our nation's public schools. Of course, such an attitude is understandable given the technocratic view of education and schooling that is predominant in our society. Ann Watts Pailliottet and Thomas Callister point out that

> by making the educational process technical, we pattern the curriculum after a stair-step model of linear fact-by-fact learning, trivialize teaching as a series of generic "how to's" or formulaic "hints and tips," and too often reduce the act of learning to simple models of behavioral stimulus-response mechanisms. (Kincheloe, Steinberg, and Villaverde 1999, 166)

The problem with this conception of education is that it reduces the teacher's role to that of identifying and managing technical problems. Pailliottet and Callister argue correctly that this view not only fails to prepare new teachers for the realities they will face in contemporary schools and society, it also undermines the attempt to foster teachers who are reflective, compassionate, and ethically minded practitioners. Moreover, the technocratic view of education is in stark contradiction to how most experienced teachers conceptualize their role and work.

Experienced teachers typically describe teaching as a very complex and intellectual *challenge* that cannot be reduced to a bag of tricks or a number of proven techniques. Indeed, much of what makes someone a good teacher, like enthusiasm in the class and compassion for students, has very little to do with technique and may not even be teachable. The point is that it is crucial to encourage our students to think less in terms of teaching recipes and more in terms of educational challenges. That is, we need to deconstruct our students' false assumption that good teaching involves merely the mastery of certain pedagogical skills. They need to realize that teaching is more like a craft or an art that involves constantly challenging oneself with new goals and ideas. As Joe Kincheloe and Shirley Steinberg assert, "nothing is simple about teaching people to think critically; no set of easy steps can be delineated in some workshop conducted by an expert in educational psychology charging twelve thousand dollars per day" (Kincheloe, Steinberg, and Villaverde 1999, 166).

In arguing that good teaching cannot be reduced to a recipe or a set of skills, my intent is neither to denigrate technique nor to imply that good teachers do not rely on various techniques in their work. My critique is aimed rather at the technocratic mindset that continues to dominate the educational system and is obsessed with questions of means, procedures, and mechanical skills. In this context it is interesting to note that the English word *technique* is derived from the Greek term *techne*, which means art or craft. For the Ancient Greeks it was clear that the mastery of any art or craft, including the art of teaching, involves acquiring certain techniques and skills. Yet both Plato and Aristotle were aware that these techniques are merely the means or methods used by the artist in the service of the fundamental goals of the different arts. They held that the artist, unlike the person with only practical experience, possesses the theoretical knowledge of their craft and is able to think deeply about issues such as relations of cause and effect.[1] A close examination of the current discussions about "standards" and the educational reform initiatives they have produced indicates that this ancient hierarchy has been greatly distorted. Technique is no longer regarded as merely a necessary condition for achieving the aims of education; it has now been elevated to the status of one of the most important educational goals.[2]

TEACHING AS RECIPE

To get a better understanding of the distinction between the "teaching-as-recipe" and the "teaching-as-challenge" models, it is fruitful to look at some of their underlying assumptions. By the teaching-as-recipe model I mean a way of conceptualizing teaching based on a mechanistic worldview and a Behaviorist educational psychology. This is a very narrow approach to education in that it asserts that a highly complex and nuanced activity like teaching can be understood if we break it down to its constituent parts and then piece them together according to causal laws. According to this view, good teachers are those who are effective at managing their classroom and preparing students to take the standardized tests. Students in such classrooms are expected to be quiet, obedient, and passive consumers of the knowledge possessed by the teacher, not active agents who can interpret ideas and create new meaning in light of their own experiences and prior knowledge.

Paulo Freire calls this model "the banking concept of education" and claims that it reduces the teacher's role to that of a depositor of information. Students, in this model, are viewed as containers who are merely expected to receive, file, store, and recall the teacher's deposits. The problem with this approach to education is that it sacrifices precisely those qualities like creativity, inquiry, and transformation that make us truly human. Freire (1994, 53) contends that ultimately

> it is the people themselves who are filed away through the lack of creativity, transformation, and knowledge in this (at best) misguided system. For apart from inquiry, apart from the praxis, individuals cannot be truly human. Knowledge emerges only through invention and re-invention, through the restless, impatient, continuing, hopeful inquiry human beings pursue in the world, with the world, and with each other.

Freire states correctly that in the banking concept of education (what I have called the teaching-as-recipe model), knowledge is viewed as a set of facts, names, dates, and formulae that the teacher needs to pass on to students. In other words, knowledge is understood as an object or a possession that some people have and some people do not. Such a conception of knowledge assumes that the world is a static reality that is not susceptible to change, new beginnings, and re-creation. Historical events, like the founding of the United States, are considered undisputable facts that are not open to debate or subject to conflicting interpretations. Likewise, scientific theories are regarded, not as particular perspectives on the natural world, but as comprehensive and infallible accounts of various phenomena in physics, chemistry, and biology. Given the fact that not only ambiguities and controversies but also feeling and fantasy are generally eliminated from the curriculum, it is not surprising that so many students lose interest in subjects like history, English, math, and the sciences. The following narrative written by a teacher educator captures this point well.

> Take black holes, for instance. I have sat in the back of classrooms where students read aloud from science textbooks describing black holes as if they were potholes. Only someone steeped in the theory of eternal return could pay attention to that text without terror. Neither text nor teacher acknowledged or questioned the horror of the relentless destruction, the great cavernous suction that the text described. I looked around the classroom. The only terrified person was me. The seventh graders, even those taking notes, seemed isolated from the text, from the world, and from the universe that it described. Black holes were in the assigned chapter with five questions at the end of it to be done for homework. The questions merely mimicked the chapter prose, so they could be answered without having even to imagine a black hole, let alone worry about one. All the kids had to do was scan the pages to find the black hole paragraph and copy out the appropriate sentences for answers. (Kincheloe and Steinberg 1995, 18)

Given what we know about the negative consequences of the teaching-as-recipe model, why do so many teachers still rely on this approach? Several reasons immediately come to mind. First, the recipe model is relatively easy to follow and use because it relies on a very structured, uniform, step-by-step approach to teaching. The formal lessons plans that are provided to teachers by schools and the boards of education are a perfect example of recipes. Such lesson plans are usually very explicit, specifying the objectives and content of the lesson, the preferred methods of instruction, as well as how much time the teacher should spend on each topic. Thus they make it much easier for teachers, especially new ones, to plan their lessons without having to think too deeply about the underlying purpose of the lesson or how to get the kids engaged in the subject. Of course, the problem with using these standard lesson plans is that teachers' creativity and critical thinking are compromised, much like that of the students who are subjected to these fixed and prescribed curricula. I was recently informed by some of my graduate students that, in order to make sure that they get a favorable evaluation during an observation, they were encouraged by their colleagues to repeat, to the same class, a lesson they had already taught. Even if such misguided tactics enable teachers to look good in the eyes of their supervisors, they turn teaching into a stale and boring activity for themselves *and* their poor students who are subjected to the same recipe twice.

Another reason for the predominance of the recipe model is that many novice and veteran teachers were themselves taught using this model. Research indicates that teachers tend to replicate the teaching approaches they themselves were exposed to as students. There is also the fact that since the recipe model calls on teachers to be the sole locus of authority, it is probably easier for them to establish and maintain discipline using this model. Indeed, many new teachers are instructed by the school administration to establish firm control of their classes before they begin teaching. Lastly, and of crucial importance, is the issue of the conditions under which teachers work. By conditions I mean things like class size, 40-minute lessons, and the enormous pressures placed on teachers to teach to the tests. The point is that these adverse conditions compel teachers, many of whom would choose other approaches, to rely on a recipe model of teaching because they lack the time, resources, and support needed to teach in a more creative and individualized way.

TEACHING AS CHALLENGE

In contrast to the teaching-as-recipe model, the teaching-as-challenge model is based on an existentialist worldview and some of the insights of critical pedagogy. Existentialists like Martin Buber maintain not only that every person is a unique being in this world but that "every living situation has, like a new born child, a new face, that has never been before and will never come again" (Buber 1955, 114). Taking Buber's assertion seriously means that we acknowledge that each student and every classroom situation is different and unique. The implication is that teachers should not react to something that arises in their classes by simply applying a given recipe that they learned from a colleague or in the teacher education program. That is, good teaching implies that we respond to these situations in a distinct and personal way. William Ayers (1995, 5-6) recognizes this point when he writes that

> the first and most fundamental challenge to teachers is to see each student in a full and complete way as possible. Students are not inert pieces of clay to be molded by clever teachers, and learning is not primarily the passive ingestion of information. If this were the case, becoming a teacher would be simple indeed. But learning requires assent, desire, action; it is characterized by discovery and surprise. And students are learning all the time — experiencing the world, organizing, reorganizing, acting, sorting, constructing, and reconstructing knowledge.

In addition, critical theorists like Freire have helped me realize that human beings do not operate outside of history and the social context, and that our identities are greatly influenced by the existing power structures in society. In the context of education, this means that many teachers work in schools in which the sheer number of students, the schedule of classes, and the irrelevant curricula (to mention only a few factors) diminish the likelihood of teachers getting to know their students. In short, the conditions under which teachers work undermine their attempt to be creative and to promote effective learning. Given these conditions, it is not surprising that many teachers view themselves as powerless. As Ayers (1995, 78) puts it,

> They tend to see themselves as relatively powerless — in relation to the negative external forces against which they must struggle, and in relation to the internal authority exerted over them by the system. Teachers know that many students come from homes that aren't particularly supportive of education, or where the youngsters receive little support of any kind. They realize that it is difficult to sustain much academic momentum and effort in children who are hungry, or who return daily to a physically unsafe environment, or who are emotionally starved or otherwise abused. Under such conditions, efforts to educate are an uphill struggle, and it is not surprising that teachers feel powerless.

Taking the insights of Buber and Freire together, we can see that teaching is a challenge in a twofold sense: It is a great challenge for teachers to respond to each student and every situation in the class-room in a unique way, and it is no less of a challenge for teachers to con-tend with some of the difficult pressures and conditions of their work. These challenges require teachers to exhibit qualities like creativity, spontaneity, imagination, presence, courage, and self-awareness. Given the numerous problems that teachers face in their classrooms ev-ery day and the qualities required by the teacher to respond to them, it is clear that the recipe model of teaching is not adequate to make sense of what it means to be a good teacher. In contrast, the challenge model associates good teaching with those qualities mentioned above, as well as passion, flexibility, and the ability to listen to children. The advan-tage of this conception of teaching is that it enables us to avoid the dan-gerous tendency to reduce the teacher's role to that of disseminating information, managing their classrooms, and preparing students to take standardized tests. Indeed, it dignifies teachers' role and profes-sion at a time when they are coming under increasing attack by politi-cians, administrators, and the general public.

In the summer of 2002, I had a unique experience that reinforced my belief that teaching should be viewed as a challenge. The class I taught was a graduate seminar in "Pedagogy and Curriculum" at Brooklyn College. It was a five-week intensive course that met Tuesdays, Wednes-days, and Thursdays for three and a half hours. Teaching about four courses a semester in the past five years, including summers, I remember feeling very weary before beginning this class. I felt like I needed a break from teaching to replenish my energy and creativity. So initially I had agreed to teach this course only for the extra income it provided. Fortu-nately, the students taking this seminar were a diverse group of people who were exceedingly lively in our class discussions. They kept me on my toes throughout the five-week course, constantly challenging my views and asking me questions I had not thought about before. After class, while riding the subway and train back home at night, I would re-flect back on the lesson we had just finished, especially on the things that I was dissatisfied with. Often I would come back the next day and begin the class by amending or qualifying something I had said the previous evening. I constantly revised my lesson plans in response to how the stu-dents were reacting to the content and the pedagogy. About midway through the course, a student who did not appear to be very involved in the class approached me with an idea to include a simulation of actual classroom management issues in the class. That night I pondered over his idea for many hours and the next day I came back to class ready to implement it with the help of this student and others. The simulation turned out to be not only hilarious but also stimulating for the students and myself. The students had an opportunity to act out and reflect on realistic scenarios that came from their own teaching experiences. And I had a chance to model for them how teachers can let go of the need to control their classrooms, which was one of the main themes of this course. I came out of this experience reinvigorated and with a new sense of commitment to continue striving to be a better teacher.

Given the numerous advantages of the teaching-as-challenge model, why has it not been embraced by most educational policymakers, leaders, and administrators? One reason is that it is much more difficult to manage and evaluate teachers' performance using a challenge model than it is using a recipe model. It is fairly simple to assess and quantify how well teachers are doing their job when they are primarily expected to control their classrooms and prepare students to take standardized tests. In contrast, when the expectation is for teachers to foster creativity, critical thinking, and citizens who are caring human beings, it is not so easy to assess whether these goals have been achieved. For the sake of efficiency and control, then, we reduce teachers' work to those qualities that are most easily measured and disregard the less tangible ones that truly distinguish the outstanding teacher from the mediocre one.

Another reason that the teaching-as-challenge model has not been more widely adopted is that the United States is a profoundly anti-intellectual society, one that puts a premium on consumerism and short-term gains. Intellectuals in general and teachers in particular are not really appreciated and taken seriously as people who have something of value to contribute to society. Indeed, sports figures, actors, musicians, and celebrities in general are regarded much more than intellectuals largely because the former generate more capital than the latter. In short, there is a huge conflict between the profit-driven, competitive culture that permeates American society and the teaching-as-challenge model that emphasizes the intellectual and scholarly nature of the profession. In a society that evaluates everything in terms of the amount of revenue that it can produce, the struggle for teachers to be recognized as intellectuals and as people who strive to make a difference in the lives of children is an uphill battle.

THE CHALLENGES OF TEACHING

Teachers need to become scholars not only of their subject matter but also of their students and of pedagogy itself. But why is it so important for teachers to become scholars or researchers? Let me begin by addressing the need for teachers to be subject matter scholars. Our current information age is radically different from those that preceded it. Not only is the magnitude of information, ideas, and knowledge in general incomparable to that of earlier generations, but also the kinds of knowledge systems at our disposal have dramatically changed. In addition to traditional print sources like books, there are now media sources such as television and videos and electronic sources such as the Internet. Thus, it is a challenge for teachers to be able to obtain and make sense of the huge amount of information out there and to analyze and make use of the different types of existing knowledge-delivery systems. Kincheloe and Steinberg are correct when they insist that becoming familiar with the different types of knowledge that exist today is a rigorous intellectual task. Such an effort, they write,

> is a content based, discursively savvy, complex analytical educational process that requires a deep understanding of a wide variety of knowledge systems, the skills to critique them, and the cognitive facility to develop new insights to replace inadequate academic constructs. (Kincheloe, Steinberg, and Villaverde 1999, 242)

To claim that teachers in general and particularly kindergarten teachers need to become scholars of their subject area might strike some people as odd or even absurd. Yet I believe they must. William Ayers points to some of the intellectual challenges of teaching young children when he writes that

> taking their ideas and their questions and their interests seriously can lead a teacher toward deep and sustained inquiry into, say, penguins and popcorn and puddles, the production of chewing gum and cheddar cheese, the politics of playgrounds or the history of parks, the physics of hackey sacks or the chemistry of hotcakes. (Ayers 1995, 1)

Ayers's examples illustrate the point that if teachers wish to engage their students in the learning process, they also need to become researchers of the topics they are teaching.

The second challenge facing teachers is to become scholars or re-searchers of their students. This means that teachers ought to get to know their students well: their backgrounds, cultures, interests, and talents, as well as their struggles and weaknesses. Getting to know one's students is no simple task, especially when many teachers in our public secondary schools are required to teach 150 students or more. Such a task is compounded today by the fact that teachers find themselves faced with an increasingly diverse student population. Gregory Michie (1999, 85) depicts the challenge in these words:

> To begin to have a true respect for my kids, I had to get to know them not only as individuals, but also as people in a particular context: children of Mexican immigrants, living in a working-class neighborhood, on the Southside of Chicago, within an increasingly xenophobic larger society, in the 1990s. I also had to commit myself to learning more about the historical, political, and economic developments — both in Mexico and in the U.S. — that had brought them to where they were, and the current issues that continued to affect them. I couldn't teach kids to honor and respect their rich legacy as Mexicans and as working people if I only did so in vague terms myself.

Michie's example and teacher research in general clearly indicate that teachers who get to know their students well have a much better chance of making a significant impact on their lives compared to those who do not.

Related to the intellectual challenge of getting to know one's students is the need to become familiar with various theories of child development as well as the social, historical, and cultural contexts in which these theories were created. It is common knowledge today that the physical, intellectual, emotional, and moral development of children affects their learning. One cannot possible understand the different ways in which children learn without having a solid awareness of how they develop. Jean Piaget, for instance, has provided us with a particularly insightful theory that explains how children develop cognitively and socially, and how learning can be used in a way that corresponds to and reinforces their cognitive and social development. Of course, any theory of child development is shaped by the particular social, historical, and cultural context in which the theorist lived and worked. Thus, Piaget's model reflects some of the interests and biases that were common among white, middle class, Western Europeans in the twentieth century. Becoming familiar with Piaget's theory as well as the context in which it was produced is a complex intellectual task, but it is one that teachers must take on in order to enhance student learning.

Third, teachers need to become researchers and scholars of pedagogy, the art of teaching. The call for teachers to become researchers of pedagogy is connected to the need for teachers to get to know their students well. Many of us were educated by teachers who did not take the time to get to know us and relied essentially on one method of instruction for all students. However, the challenge for teachers to get to know their students implies that they first recognize that not all students learn in the same way or at the same pace. Acknowledging this fact suggests that teachers will have to learn a number of different instructional methods that can be used to teach students who have differing learning styles, interests and abilities. The notion that students have what Howard Gardner calls multiple intelligences requires teachers to become researchers and scholars of diverse approaches to teaching and learning.

Moreover, it is important to keep in mind that every approach to teaching and learning was constructed in a particular social-historical context that gave it meaning. In order to fully understand these approaches, teachers will need to explore this context, including the beliefs and assumptions that were common then. John Dewey's views on education, for instance, truly make sense only if we keep in mind that he formulated them in the context of the rise of modern science and the belief that scientific inquiry was the way to bring about social progress. In my foundation classes I call this undertaking "the practice of making the implicit explicit." The point that I try to get across to future teachers is that it is absolutely crucial for them to make explicit the underlying assumptions of various historical pedagogical theories as well as their own views of education. Students who are never encouraged to examine their basic assumptions all too often come to accept the theories and views they subscribe to as "natural," inevitable, and unchangeable. When these students become teachers they will most likely find ways to adjust to the existing state of schooling in America and become supporters of the status quo. Only rarely will they gain the insights and critical abilities that will enable them to become transforming agents and educational reformers.

Conclusion

Teaching needs to be conceived as a very complex and intricate challenge rather than merely following recipes created by others. Thus I strenuously oppose the attempts among many educators to limit the teachers' role to transferring information and mastering various classroom management techniques. Yet why is it so important to insist on this point now? One reason is that education and teaching have been reduced in many public debates and schools to a technical endeavor to find the most efficient means to achieve a set of prescribed ends. For example, in the recent discussions on standards and educational reform, the fundamental questions about the nature and purpose of education have been largely ignored. As Jeffrey Kane notes, "the question now is one of means and means alone: how to provide educational experiences that effectively enable children to achieve the desired goals" (Kane 1998, 2).

Moreover, Kane claims that the underlying epistemological, moral, ontological, and economic foundations of the new standards are taken for granted rather than debated. Since all efforts are aimed at discovering the most efficient methods of attaining these standards, there is almost no discussion taking place about crucial issues such as "what learning means to the learner in terms of the way he/she develops an understanding of self, other, and the world" (Kane 1998, 3). My experience as well as that of many other teacher educators indicates that if we do not challenge our students to engage such questions, they easily fall into the trap of equating teaching with being a good technician. They may be skilled at writing formal lesson plans and controlling their classes, but know very little about what a worthy education means and how to cultivate it.

One of my students has beautifully captured the notion of teaching as a challenge.

> I used to say that I loved to teach and I truly did think that.
> When I was a child I used to place empty chairs and pretend to
> teach invisible students. At the age of thirteen, I taught my
> younger sister (who was three) to read, write, and do math.
> She skipped kindergarten because she was too advanced. I
> also enjoyed tutoring children at the church. It made me happy
> and gave me a great feeling of satisfaction when others did
> better on a test. Then it made me think: I could do this thing,
> teach. It is my forté, my talent, my joie de vivre. I enjoyed it.

However, teaching high school has been quite an experience. Faced with approximately 150 teenagers per day is enough to make anyone tear their hair out (Mine is turning gray). It seems to me that I could never get enough done. Their snide remarks take 15% of the lesson time. They test you every day in some way or other. They walk in without books, paper, pens (I never knew I had to be everyone's mother). They try to concoct all kinds of ways to get out of class. "My stomach is hurting, I've got to go to the nurse." They stand before you knock-kneed, twisting in every direction: "Ms. Wilson, I've got to go to the bathroom."

I should be focusing on content at that level, not the human factor. The assumption is that by now they have already been taught to be humans and, therefore, now, all we have to teach is the subject. Nevertheless, the challenge for me every day is what can I do to improve the human factor so that I can get through the content in a given period of time.

The human factor in teaching is something I had never really considered when I thought I had teaching talent or ability. Now I find myself questioning whether I am a good teacher! What is a good teacher anyway? The ability to just explain the subject? Or is it the ability to get it across to your students and make it somehow relevant to their lives? Or is it turning your students into good people who are willing to learn the subject and achieve? Sure it was OK to teach my little sister and countless others whom I had known all of my life. But teaching others with different backgrounds, levels of aptitude, education, personality, trying to teach 150 teenage individuals is mind-boggling.

Is it enough to teach the child who lives in a drug-infested area Math 1 or 2? His daily human experience is witnessing others taking drugs and well-dressed dealers with flashy looking cars. In terms of math, the dealer pulls out wads of bills before him and buys whatever he wants. One way or the other this will affect his character. Maybe he or she sees school as a waste of time. After all, what does he or she do? Sit every day in a math class learning geometry, wondering how these calculations are supposed to get him or her flashy cars and a wad of bills. How do I tie it all in with the math, his daily experience? Shouldn't I touch the person before I teach him or her? Wouldn't this make him or her want to listen more intently, and therefore learn?

It becomes a fight of wills, and I don't believe I am going to win. Somehow I have to win these students over. I have to show them what is in my heart. I want them to pass brilliantly. I want them to take their potentially bright futures and make it a reality. But I cannot do this without their participation. I have to show them that teaching is a partnership, not an absolute rule thing.

This is the challenge I face every day. They are just kids. However, every time they walk into the classroom, they and I hold a small yet big part of their futures in our hands. That's not kid stuff. I now know that my ability to deal with people may be just as important as explaining or communicating subject matter.

I strongly believe that teacher education programs must be committed to cultivating teachers who, like Ms. Wilson, are able to ask philosophical questions, doubt and critically reflect on education in general and on what they are doing daily in their classes. Like Ms. Wilson, we need teachers who do not have all the "answers" but who are struggling to find their own voices (identities) in schools in which conformity to established norms, methods, and subject matter is the rule. Schools of education must foster teachers who are aware of the social, political, and cultural embeddedness of the education system and how it affects them and students from different backgrounds. Above all, we need teachers who, like Ms. Wilson, approach their vocation as a challenge and are determined to make a difference in the lives of their students.

NOTES

1. Following the example of the Greeks, the word *art* is used here in the broad sense to refer not only to the fine arts but also to the productive arts, like carpentry and architecture, as well as to the service arts such as medicine and teaching. For Aristotle's conception of art, see Richard McKeon's General Introduction in *Introduction to Aristotle*, edited by Richard McKeon (1947).

2. In the current "educational standards reform initiative" of the State of New York, schools of education are required to prepare teachers to "teach their prospective students *how to* write and perform various other literacy skills." While fostering literacy is undoubtedly an important education goal, the State's guidelines emphasize the technical aspect of teaching and learning literacy with little regard to questions like the meaning of literacy, its underlying purpose, or the cultural context in which it takes place.

Chapter Two

Theories Can Be Applied Directly to Practice

> I came to theory because I was hurting — the pain within me
> was so intense that I could not go on living. I came to theory
> desperate, wanting to comprehend — to grasp what was hap-
> pening around and within me. Most importantly, I wanted to
> make the hurt go away. I saw in theory then a location for
> healing. (hooks 1994, 59)

One of the most difficult challenges facing teachers, college professors, and scholars in general is the task of relating theory to practice. A
conception, shared by many new teachers, is that the theories they learn
in their education classes have little to do with the issues and problems
that come up in their own classrooms. I believe that there are many reasons for the perceived mismatch between theory and practice, philosophy and action.[1] One obvious reason, as bell hooks points out, is the way
theories are often used by groups of scholars to distinguish and isolate
themselves from the general public. hooks (1994, 64) writes that

> it is evident that one of the many uses of theory in academic
> locations is in the production of an intellectual class hierarchy
> where the only work deemed truly theoretical is work that is
> highly abstract, jargonistic, difficult to read, and containing
> obscure references.

Since such theories are inaccessible to a wide audience, they are often
deemed useless and alienating by the very people they are designed to

help. As such, they create a huge gap between theory and practice that
serves to perpetuate class elitism. Like bell hooks, I believe that any theory that cannot be shared in everyday language cannot be used to educate the public.

Another reason for the conflict between theory and practice is related
to the conditions under which teachers work. Many public school teachers work in situations in which they are closely supervised and controlled, leaving them with little power and autonomy to make crucial
educational decisions that affect themselves and their students. Issues
such as the content of the curriculum, the methods of instruction, the organization of time and of classrooms are not left to the discretion of
teachers but are handled by administrators, policymakers, and so-called
experts. As a result, teachers spend most of their time trying to follow the
instructions of others in order to survive, rather than thinking and theorizing about what they are doing and how they are doing it. In this sad
state of affairs in which teachers are required to merely follow the prescriptions of others, it is not surprising that the gulf between educational
theory and the practice of teaching becomes even wider.

In what follows I take up the view shared by many teachers that the
educational theories they learned are so far removed from the problems
they face daily in their classrooms that they are irrelevant. However, my
analysis focuses on a different aspect of this mismatch between theory
and practice: the misleading notion that an educational theory can just
be taken in its entirety and plugged into a particular classroom. Such
misconception fails to take into account the meaning and power of theories, as well as the social-historical context in which educational theories
are created. What we often fail to realize is that there are alternative ways
of applying educational insights to one's teaching.

THE MEANING AND POWER OF THEORY

The Greek term *theoria* from which our word *theory* is derived con-
notes viewing or contemplating. The modern meaning of this term usually refers to a "statement or set of statements offered to explain a
phenomenon. It is a way of organizing ideas to provide a more complete
understanding of what the data indicate in a piecemeal fashion" (Zigler
and Stevenson 1993, 47). A theory is essentially a detailed account of a
particular aspect of reality whether in physics, chemistry, biology, medicine, psychology, sociology, or education. It is a way of organizing and
making sense of data in each of these disciplines from a specific vantage

point. This means that theories should not be considered undisputable facts or definite truths but rather one among many ways of explaining a given phenomenon. Indeed, in each of the sciences there are often competing theories that attempt to account for the same phenomena. The history of science indicates that as more evidence was discovered to support innovative theories, they gradually came to be accepted by the scientific community. At the same time, the older theories steadily lost their credibility and popularity and were sometimes even forgotten.

All people, including children, engage in theorizing, meaning that they constantly observe and try to make sense of the world around them. Experienced teachers who discuss with colleagues the ideas, goals, and methods they have found successful in their classes are theorizing. They are constructing a theory[2] to explain what they did with their students, how they did it, what they were trying to achieve, and why they believe it worked or did not work. Educational theory is, therefore, often aimed at clarifying and justifying some kind of practice or action that teachers are engaged in. The practice of teaching, on the other hand, provides the context, material, and testing ground for educational theory. In teaching, there is no doubt that theory and practice are interrelated — each influences and is influenced by the other.

Despite this close connection between theory and practice in education, when I was a graduate student at Teachers College, the practice of teaching was rarely, if ever, discussed in my classes. It was assumed, I suppose, that "Ivy League" graduate students are generally not interested in questions of practice and if they are, they can make the connections between theory and practice themselves, after class. I strongly reject this approach. Following educators like John Dewey, I believe that theory and practice, philosophy and action, are interrelated and that it is the teacher's responsibility to make their connections explicit. Throughout my college teaching experiences in Israel, Brooklyn College, and Quinnipiac University, I have discovered again and again that students of education frequently find it very difficult to make these connections on their own. Thus, in my courses, I not only give many examples that illustrate the relationships between theory and practice, I also require students to practice making such connections in virtually all the assignments they do. In this way, the students are constantly required to reflect on the connections of theory and practice with the hope that they come to realize that our philosophies shape the way in which we conduct our classrooms and that our educational experiences often help us revise and refine our theories of teaching and learning.

To be sure, many of my students openly ask me to make these connections explicit and they constantly raise questions that indicate that they are trying to make sense of this issue. How else is it possible for students of education to fully comprehend the things they are doing daily in the classroom? Dewey (1966, 275) argues quite convincingly that if modern science has demonstrated anything,

> it is that there is no such thing as genuine knowledge and fruitful understanding except as the offspring of *doing*. The analysis and arrangement of facts which is indispensable to the growth of knowledge and power of explanation and right classification cannot be obtained purely mentally — just inside the head. Men have to *do* something to the things when they wish to find out something; they have to alter conditions.

Thus, as Dewey asserts, it is only by experimenting with various teaching techniques and practices that teachers are able to gain genuine knowledge about teaching and learning, knowledge that is tangible and comprehensible to them.

On the other hand, it is theories that can provide teachers with an awesome power to analyze and assess what they and the schools are doing in the often harsh realities of public schools. bell hooks (1994, 61) makes this point very well:

> Living in childhood without a sense of home, I found a place of sanctuary in "theorizing," in making sense out of what was happening. I found a place where I could imagine possible futures, a place where life could be lived differently. This "lived" experience of critical thinking, of reflection and analysis, became a place where I worked at explaining the hurt and making it go away. Fundamentally, I learned from this experience that theory could be a healing place.

Drawing on hooks's insights, we can see that only by theorizing are teachers able to interpret and make sense of the difficulties they encounter in their classes and schools. Theories provide teachers with a frame of reference and a language with which to name and critically analyze many of the problems they face daily. However, as hooks points out, theory is also a place of hope and healing. That is, theories provide teachers with a rich source of understanding not only of what *is*, but also of how things could be differently. Teachers and educators in general who are struggling to make a difference need to become theorists who can imagine and create alternatives to many of the oppressive ideologies, practices, and conditions found in America's public schools today.

THE CHALLENGES OF APPLYING THEORY TO PRACTICE

In the section above I argued that theories help teachers evaluate and put in perspective not only what they *are* doing but also what they *should be* doing in their work with students. Yet despite theories' very important function in education, many new teachers cannot easily see the value in theorizing. Even when teachers find the things they are learning in class inspirational, they tend to regard theories as ideal and unrelated to the "real" world of classrooms and schools. Here is how one student teacher (Ayers 1995, 195) describes this predicament:

> Student teaching is a strange thing. Unfortunately, it is a very quick jump into reality. And for me and my friends, it is a jump that hasn't been pleasant. Our wonderful TE [teacher education] classes were inspirational and very interesting, but the reality of school and teaching [in many elementary schools] is much different. There are daily problems, interruptions, politics, restrictions, and situations that make it nearly impossible to teach the way we believe.

My own students at Brooklyn College, most of which were already teaching, constantly voiced the same sentiment; they could not easily see the connection between the theories we studied and the reality of their own classrooms. For example, when I asked students last summer in my seminar in Pedagogy and Curriculum to evaluate the course at the end of the semester, I received responses like: "This course is very ivory tower," or "The theories we learned are great and positive but not realistic for New York City teachers." These students seem to have accepted the widespread notion that educational theories can just be taken in their entirety and put into practice. They assume that a

> *good* theory should be directly applicable to practical life —
> that it can be "plugged" into actual situations and yield direct

results. If the theory does not work, then it is a *bad* theory. This
assumption may be the reason that many people show disdain for theory and call it impractical, for few if any educational theories can be applied directly to practical conditions
in the sense that one applies aspirin to a headache. (Ozmon
and Craver 1999, 9)

This misconception, I believe, is related to a failure to appreciate the
meaning and power of theories. I mentioned earlier that a theory
should not be confused with an absolute fact; it is rather one among
many possible ways of explaining a given phenomenon. Such explanations, or ideas that are organized in some coherent structure, are themselves open to interpretation and can usually be viewed from more
than one perspective. However, some perspectives give us a dimmer or
narrower rather than a clearer or more complex picture of what we are
trying to understand. For example, when reading and discussing educational theories in my classes, my students will frequently attempt to
interpret them literally. Literal interpretations lead many of my students to conclude that the ideas they are learning (from Socrates to bell
hooks) are impractical and therefore insignificant for them. Yet, when
these same students are encouraged to consider the symbolic rather
than the literal meaning of these theories, they generally arrive at a new
understanding of the ideas and are able to see how they can be applied
in their lives and work.

Symbolic or metaphorical interpretations give us insight into texts
that, like dreams, rarely make sense if we consider them literally.
When I have shown the movie *Harold and Maude* in my class and asked
students to talk about the approach to education that Maude represents, many of them have responded by referring to Maude as simply
"a crazy old woman with no respect for the law." This literal perspective prevents these students from viewing Maude as a symbol of free
spirit and active resistance to conformity to established norms. Once
my students take this symbolic viewpoint, they are able to recognize
that Maude's message has deep significance for them in the context of
a system of education in which conformity to established norms,
methods, and subject matter is the rule. In this way students not only
gain a deeper understanding of the movie, but are able to make connections between some of its insights and their own daily struggles in
the public schools.

The point that I wish to stress here is that many teachers' disdain of theory is due in part to their conception that good theories are settled facts that have direct applicability to their classrooms. If, on the other hand, theories are viewed as guides to thought and instruments of interpretation, it becomes clear that they cannot simply be "plugged in" to a particular classroom. Similarly, to argue, as I have, that theory and practice are interrelated does not mean that there is a direct or causal connection between the two, as though one could simply apply a given theory to a classroom situation like one applies a proven remedy to a disease. Instead, the interrelation of theory and practice implies that they are mutually dependent, that each can inform and be used to evaluate the other. The significance of theory is in its ability to define the problems that teachers face, clarify their confusions, and to suggest possible solutions to these problems.

The misconception among teachers that theories can be directly applied to their classes is also related to a failure to appreciate theories as social-historical constructs. Every theory was created in a particular social, historical, political, and economic context that helped to shape the ideas that make up the theory. Indeed, one cannot fully comprehend the philosophies of Rousseau, Dewey, Freire, or any one else for that matter, without taking into account the context in which they were formulated. Paulo Freire, for instance, first developed his philosophy of education in *Pedagogy of the Oppressed,* a book he wrote at the end of the 1960s in the context of the poor and illiterates of northeastern Brazil. When Freire was asked about how the insights of this book can be integrated in early childhood education in the United States, he made it clear that his educational philosophy cannot simply be applied to a completely different context in a gridlike fashion. Rather, he insisted, that if one wished to adapt his ideas on education to a different context, they must first be *reformulated* to address the specific needs and conditions of this particular context. The fact that educational theories are not universal truths but historical products that were created in particular contexts, implies that we must be extremely cautious when we try to apply a theory that was created to meet the needs of one situation to a completely different set of circumstances.

RELATING THEORY TO PRACTICE

The fact that educational theories cannot be simply "plugged" into classroom situations or applied directly to practice does not mean that they are not relevant to the life and work of teachers. Indeed, theories are great resources that help teachers analyze the problems they encounter in their classes and schools and suggest possibilities for improvement. Yet, what are some of the concrete ways in which teachers can apply the theories they have learned and embrace to their teaching? In the rest of this chapter I would like to develop the notion of applied theory and suggest alternative ways of making theories relevant and practical for teachers. Specifically, I will propose four ways in which theories can be applied to the classroom. My contention is not that these are the *only* ways in which educational theories can be applied to teachers' work and my hope is that my analysis will provoke educators to reflect on other, more personal ways of making theories relevant.

APPLYING PARTS OR ASPECTS OF A THEORY

One way in which educational theories can be relevant for the classroom is when teachers integrate parts or aspects of a theory in their work. Here I am making a distinction between a theory of education in its entirety and particular insights that make up the theory. Throughout history thinkers have developed fairly complex and comprehensive theories that attempt to explain general educational issues, such as the nature of human beings and knowledge, the meaning of teaching and learning, the purpose of education, and so forth. While it is not feasible to take a theory as a whole and plug it into a particular classroom, it is possible to take specific insights or aspects of a theory and integrate them into one's teaching. For instance, consider Rousseau's notion that all children have various "natural" inclinations or tendencies and that a worthy education has to cultivate rather than repress these inclinations. This insight and those of other educators and psychologists have taught us that children, especially young ones, need to be able to move about and be active and that we cannot expect them to sit and just listen for extended periods of time. Rousseau's idea that children have a basic need to be active and explore their surroundings has had a profound impact on the way in which early childhood and elementary classrooms are organized and run. Many of these classrooms are divided into various centers in which children have the opportunity to construct knowledge through hands-on activities and the use of their senses. Based on Rousseau's insight, children in such classrooms learn primarily by exploring and experimenting with various stimuli rather than by passively absorbing the information that the teacher transmits.

Dewey's notion that the child and the curriculum should be viewed as interrelated and as mutually dependent elements of the learning process is another aspect of a theory that can be applied to one's teaching. Taking issue with both traditional education that focused mainly on the curriculum and with a child-centered approach that emphasized the learner with his or her needs, Dewey calls on educators to explore the connections between the two. He argues that we need to find a way to bridge the gap between children's needs, experiences, and aspirations and the goals and values of society on which the formal school curriculum is based. This insight has had a huge impact on how contemporary curricula are designed as well as on the ways in which teachers present subject matter. Contemporary curricula take into account the needs of the students by including more texts that students find interesting and can to which they can relate. Thus, young-adult novels in high school English classes, "our own communities" units in elementary social studies, and different types of animals in science classes are part of the curriculum of public schools. In addition, many teachers begin their lessons today with something that the students already know or have experienced (sometimes called a "motivation" or a "hook") and they make an effort to interpret the subject matter so that it pertains to the students' lives. Taking Dewey's insight seriously that the child and the curriculum are interrelated has, in fact, resulted in better curricula and instruction and in more students being engaged in the lessons.

A Direction for Reflection and Action

Besides offering teachers specific insights that are applicable to their classrooms, theories can provide educators with a direction for reflection and action. That is, theories give educators a new way of thinking about and resolving many of the issues and problems they face every day. Martin Buber's dialogical approach to education is a good example of a theory that does this. For Buber, dialogue, or a genuine relation between two whole persons, is fundamental to what it means to be a human being. The fact that in education people constantly interact with one another implies that establishing deep relationships and dialogue will have an important role to play in this realm.

For example, Buber vividly describes an incident in which a novice teacher enters a classroom for the first time and encounters a great deal of noise, disorder, and even chaos among the students. The teacher is initially tempted, as most of us would be, to start by issuing orders and curbing this or that troublemaker. He is tempted, in other words, to start by dealing with discipline and classroom management which Buber calls "starting from beneath."

> But then his eyes meet a face which strikes him. It is not a beautiful face or particularly intelligent; but it is a real face, or rather the chaos preceding the cosmos of a real face. On it he reads a question which is something different from the general curiosity: "Who are you? Do you know something that concerns me? Do you bring me something? What do you bring?
>
> In some such way he reads the question. And he the young teacher addresses his face. He says nothing very ponderous or important, he puts an ordinary introductory question: "What did you talk about last in geography? The Dead Sea? Well, what about the Dead Sea?" But there was obviously something not quite usual in the question, for the answer he gets is not the ordinary schoolboy answer; the boy begins to *tell a story*. Some months earlier he had stayed for a few hours on the shores of the Dead Sea, and it is of this he tells. He adds: "And everything looked to me as if it had been created a day before the rest of creation." Quite unmistakably he had only in this moment made up his mind to talk about it. In the meantime his face has changed. It is no longer quite as chaotic as before. And the class has fallen silent. They all listen. The class, too, is no longer a chaos. Something has happened. The young teacher has started from above. (Buber 1955, 112-113)

This anecdote begins with a very realistic depiction of what many new teachers face when they walk into their own classrooms for the first time: disorder. And the initial temptation of this teacher, make the students settle down and then dictate the rules of appropriate conduct, is also quite common. However, as Buber's anecdote unfolds we see that the teacher begins the class not by disciplining the misbehaving students, but rather by attempting to establish a dialogue with a particular student. The dialogue that emerges between the teacher and one of the students actually starts on the non-verbal level, on the level of looks and gazes. Next the two engage in a brief question and answer dialogue culminating in the student sharing a personal story with the teacher and rest of the class. Through this dialogue, which Buber calls "starting from above," the students gradually settle down and begin to listen to the story. Thus to start from above is to start by attempting to engage the students in a meaningful dialogue on a topic that is relevant to them. It is an effort to establish a relation with a student or a number of students for the sake of gaining their trust and ultimately making an impact on their character.

What are the implications of Buber's notion of "starting from above" for the challenges that both new and experienced teachers encounter when they begin the school year? In particular, how does Buber's insight shed light on the debate about dealing with discipline problems, one of the most difficult issues that teachers face? Clearly, Buber's notion of starting from above does not imply that every teacher who walks into a disorderly classroom and tries to make eye contact and establish a relation with a particular student is going to get the same result that this teacher did. That is, Buber's insight should not be viewed as a specific prescription or recipe that should be directly applied whenever teachers encounter discipline problems. Rather, starting from above by attempting to make a connection should be conceived as an alternative way of making sense of and responding to discipline problems in the classroom. From Buber's perspective, students who are disrupting the class when a new teacher enters are not just misbehaving and showing no respect, but are probably trying to determine if they can trust this teacher. Like the students in the anecdote, they are testing the teacher to see if he or she is genuinely interested in establishing a relation with them.

The point I wish to make here is that teachers who walk into an unruly classroom should not try to copy what the teacher in the anecdote did but rather reflect on how they can establish a relation (dialogue) with their individual class. Indeed, Buber's anecdote teaches us that a dialogue between two people can manifest in many different ways including eye contact, questions and answers, an argument, and so on. Since every classroom situation is unique, the process of establishing a relation or dialogue between teachers and their students will always come about in slightly different ways that cannot be predicted in advance. The advantages of beginning the school year by trying to establish a relationship based on trust with one's students instead of by issuing orders are immense. Students are much more likely to open up to, listen to, and respect the teacher if they recognize that he or she is not trying to manipulate them but to get to know them as persons who have something of value to contribute. And teachers have a much greater chance of making a long-lasting impact on the kind of persons their students will become if they strive to create meaningful dialogues with them.

RECONSTRUCTING A THEORY TO MEET SPECIFIC CONTEXTUAL NEEDS

Every theory is a product of a particular social, historical, and political context that helped shape the ideas that make up the theory. Another way of making educational theories relevant to the practice of teaching is to *reconstruct* a theory to meet the needs of a specific context that is different from the one in which it was created. By reconstructing a theory to meet the needs of a specific context, I mean interpreting it in such a way that it can relate to the issues and problems of the new context. To illustrate this, consider how Freire's critical theory of education — or what he calls problem-posing education — can be applied to the elementary classroom.

Problem-posing education is radically different from what Freire calls the "banking concept of education," an approach to education that reduces the teacher's role to that of a depositor of information and the students to containers who are merely expected to absorb the teacher's deposits. In contrast, problem-posing education does not consist in the transferals of information but in developing the consciousness or critical thinking skills of the students. Unlike banking education, problem-posing education is based on dialogue, which means that the teacher is no longer the only one who teaches, but one who also learns through the dialogue with the students. Similarly, in this model the students take on the responsibility not only to learn but also to become co-teachers in the learning process.

The conflict between banking education and Freire's problem-posing approach reveals itself not only in the way in which the learning process is conducted but also in the content of the material. While in the banking model the content is based on facts, dates, names, formulas, and other bits of information, in problem-posing education, as its name indicates, the focus is on problems. The problems that Freire has in mind are ones that not only affect students directly but are also connected to broader social, political, economic, and moral issues. For Freire, the advantage of focusing on problems as opposed to mere facts is that students will gain a critical awareness of themselves in relation to the world. Such an awareness, he believes, will lead students to become committed to changing those oppressive realities that affect them:

Students, as they are increasingly posed with problems relating to themselves in the world and with the world, will feel
increasingly challenged and obliged to respond to that challenge. Because they apprehend the challenge as interrelated
to other problems within a total context, not as a theoretical
question, the resulting comprehension tends to be increasingly critical and thus constantly less alienated. Their response to the challenge evokes new challenges, followed by
new understandings; and gradually the students come to regard themselves as committed. (Freire 1994, 62)

Granted that this description of Freire's theory of education is sketchy,
how might we use a problem-posing approach in an elementary classroom? Suppose that we are interested in teaching "Columbus and Native American Issues," how should we approach this topic from a
Freirian perspective? Bob Peterson, a fifth grade public school teacher,
reminds us that our approach to controversial issues like this one depends on the students' developmental level. "Even the youngest children, however, should begin to experiment with words such as 'fair,'
'unfair,' and 'stereotype,' just as we try to teach them the meaning of 'respect' and 'cooperate'" (Bigelow and Peterson 1998, 35). Regarding Columbus, Peterson points out that through dramatization and discussion
children can realize that "if someone was living in their house and someone else came up and 'discovered' it, it wouldn't be fair for the new person to kick the current resident out" (Bigelow and Peterson 1998, 38). By
taking a problem that many students can relate to (being kicked out of a
house or a room) and relating it to a broader social-historical issue (the
European invasion of America), students begin to challenge the Columbus myth and gain a much deeper and more complex understanding of
this issue. Through dramatization, role-playing, discussions, songs, and
many other techniques illustrated by Peterson, a Freirian problem-posing approach can be used to teach the topic of Columbus in any elementary classroom.

Likewise, Native American issues can be taught from a Freirian perspective by focusing on various stereotypes that we associate with Native American people. Peterson suggests that we begin teaching this
topic by requesting our students to draw or write down what they know
about Native Americans. Next, the teacher should ask the students what
identifies the person in their drawing as an "Indian." Typically, the an-

swers that students give are based on stereotypes such as the teepee, feathers, and bows and arrows. Peterson observes that

> The pictures and stories will not only help teachers under-
> stand the children's stereotypes, but can be the basis for dis-
> cussion. Ask the students where they got their ideas for what
> they drew or wrote. Ask if they think the pictures or drawings
> are accurate. It's necessary to point out that some native peo-
> ple did use teepees, and that feathers played an important
> role among many Native Americans, but when we generalize
> we are stereotyping. (Bigelow and Peterson 1998, 36)

Once students understand the significance of the notion of stereotype, they can begin to see how stereotypes are used to make Indians seem inferior or less than human. Consistent with a Freirian approach to education, these activities will not only give students a deeper awareness of various Native American issues, but will also enhance their general critical thinking skills.

IDEALS FOR EVALUATING WHAT WE ARE DOING IN OUR CLASSROOMS

A fourth way in which theories can be relevant for the classroom is by providing teachers and other educators various ideals and standards for evaluating their own practice. One of bell hooks's insights illustrates how theories can be used to assess educational practices and to imagine possible alternatives to practices that are dull, stifling, and alienating. In the introduction to her book *Teaching to Transgress: Education as the Practice of Freedom*, hooks (1994, 7) writes:

> *Excitement* in higher education was viewed as potentially dis-
> ruptive of the atmosphere of seriousness assumed to be es-
> sential to the learning process. To enter classroom settings in
> colleges and universities with the will to share the desire to
> encourage excitement, was to transgress. Not only did it re-
> quire movement beyond accepted boundaries, but excite-
> ment could not be generated without a full recognition of the
> fact that there could never be an absolute set agenda govern-
> ing teaching practices. Agendas had to be flexible, had to al-
> low for spontaneous shifts in direction. Students had to be
> seen in their particularity as individuals ... and interacted

with according to their needs…. Critical reflection on my experience as a student in unexciting classrooms enabled me not only to imagine that the classroom could be exciting but that this excitement could co-exist with and even stimulate serious intellectual and/or academic engagement.

I would argue that hooks's notion of the need for excitement in higher education is equally true for all of our schools. That is, excitement and fun in public school classrooms is frequently seen as undermining the atmosphere of seriousness, conformity to rules, and standardization that permeates schools. hooks rightly challenges the belief that learning can only occur in an atmosphere that is serious, stern, and authoritarian; she insists that rigorous academic engagement is consistent with excitement in the classroom. Is it really true that for significant learning to take place, there needs to be an atmosphere of seriousness in the classroom? For example, does the fact that many teachers begin their lesson with a "do-now" activity designed to get students working as soon as they enter the class imply that more learning is taking place in such classrooms? I have observed numerous lessons that began with this kind of activity only to realize that many students did not even do the assignment, let alone engage in significant learning. In short, much of what is deemed as learning in our schools is actually an attempt to keep students busy and manage their behavior.

Moreover, teachers who have the flexibility to change their agendas and methods of instruction and create exciting learning environments have a much greater chance to motivate their students than teachers who go by the book. We also know that many students become alienated from school and learning precisely because they do not find their teachers exciting and stimulating. Typically, the teachers that we remember, the ones that made the most impact on us, are those that transgressed boundaries and challenged us intellectually while maintaining an exciting classroom environment. Hooks's ideal that learning should be exciting and even fun can be used as a standard by which we evaluate things like the content of the curriculum, the atmosphere and organization of our schools, and the activities that teachers use to stimulate learning.

CONCLUSION

The four ways I have presented in which theories can be applied to the classroom should be viewed neither as comprehensive or mutually exclusive. In fact, there is quite a bit of overlap between these four recommendations for applying theoretical insights to one's teaching. For instance, the notion that theories give us a direction for reflection and action is related to the assertion that theories provide ideals and standards for evaluating what teachers are doing in the classroom. Similarly, the suggestion that teachers can apply parts or aspects of a theory to their work is connected to the recommendation to reconstruct a theory to meet the needs of a specific content. When we take a particular insight from a theory and seek to apply it to our classrooms, we first have to reconstruct or interpret it so that it will fit the specific needs of our situation.

My intention in this chapter is not to provide another "how-to" list of four things that educators should do to make themselves better teachers. It is rather to offer teachers alternative ways of thinking about educational theory and its relationship to practice. Viewing theories as guides to thought and instruments of interpretation help us realize the numerous ways in which theory can inform and enhance the practice of teaching. In fact, in describing different ways in which educational theories can be applied to the practice of teaching, I have been engaged in the act of theorizing. Theorizing, in its applied form, is essentially interpreting ideas so that they can shed light on a practical situation. It is explaining how certain educational goals and methods can relate to something that we are already doing or could be doing in the classroom.

NOTES

1. Throughout this book, I will be using the words *theory* and *philosophy* interchangeably. Similarly, both *educational theory* and *philosophy of education* are used to refer to a comprehensive approach to education.
2. It should be made clear that I am using the word *theory* broadly to signify not only a way of explaining and making sense of educational practice but also to indicate ideals or visions for evaluating what teachers ought to be doing.

Chapter Three

Students Need to Know "The Basics"

> What is basic is not a certain set of texts, or principles or algo-
> rithms, but the conversation that makes sense of these things.
> Curriculum is that conversation. It is the process of making
> sense with a group of people of the systems that shape and or-
> ganize the world that we can think about together. (Grumet
> 1995)[1]

As a teacher educator, I constantly encourage my in-service teachers
to challenge their students to think critically and independently, to analyze, synthesize, and question ideas as opposed to merely memorizing
facts and regurgitating information. The response that I typically get
from my students goes something like this: "how can we teach children
to think without first giving them the Basics?" Embedded in this statement are some problematic assumptions about the meaning and purpose of the Basics in education. The Basics, according to this view, are a
set of essential facts, dates, names, formulas, events, and words that
need to be committed to memory in order for a person to be deemed educated. Acquiring this fragmented knowledge is then all too often associated with being an educated citizen or, at the very least, with learning the
necessary skills to compete in the global workforce.

Perhaps the most immediate problem with the assumption that
knowledge equals the ability to remember a set of factoids is that it just
does not hold up to close scrutiny. If the aim of public schooling in the
United States is to foster educated and active citizens, then we are surely
failing miserably at this task. To verify this point all you have to do is to
look at the number of eligible citizens who typically vote in national elec-

tions and, more importantly, at the fact that there is a growing culture of violence, consumption, and entertainment in the United States, but no culture of public discourse and civic action. Yet even if our aim is the more limited one of preparing students for the workforce, it is doubtful that our schools are achieving this goal. As the job market continues to become increasingly skilled and specialized and schools continue to focus on the Basics (the three R's), there is a growing concern that we are shortchanging our students, especially poor, disadvantaged, and minority students.

In questioning the value of equating education with the learning of a set of essential facts, I do not mean to suggest that there is no such thing as "the Basics" in education. Rather, the issue is how we define the Basics and what kind of role we assign them in the education of our children. Gaining a clearer sense of these questions will not only help educators foster good workers and engaged citizens, it will also enable them to cultivate students who are thoughtful and caring human beings.

THE SIGNIFICANCE OF THE BASICS

Historically speaking, there is nothing new about a concept that is repeated over and over by politicians, scholars, and ordinary people without anyone having a clear idea what it means. Such is the case when students of education claim that they cannot teach their students how to think independently and critically without first instructing them in the Basics. Similarly, when politicians and educational policymakers reproach our public schools and teachers for failing to teach students the Basics, we should stop them immediately and ask: basic for whom? For what? And in what context? The fallacy embedded in both of these claims is captured very succinctly by John Gatto (2002, 3-4) in his book *Dumbing Us Down: The Hidden Curriculum of Compulsory Schooling.*

> The logic of the school-mind is that it is better to leave school with a tool kit of superficial jargon derived from economics, sociology, natural science, and so on than with one genuine enthusiasm. But quality in education entails learning about something in depth.... Meaning, not disconnected facts, is what sane human beings seek, and education is a set of codes for processing raw data into meaning. Behind the patchwork quilt of school sequences and the school obsession with facts and theories, the age-old human search for meaning lies well concealed.

What I am getting at here is that there is a serious problem with the way the "Basics" have been conceptualized as a set of essential facts that need to be memorized. The problem is not so much that we require students to learn facts, words, and formulas in History, English and Math. The problem is the *value* we attribute to retaining these bits of information. Simply put, schools commonly confuse means with ends when they teach the Basics as a set of essential facts to be committed to memory. Rather than viewing the mastery of these facts as merely a means of attaining some higher educational purpose, memorizing information has been elevated to the level of one of the most important educational goals. If you doubt my assertions just look at how many spelling quizzes teachers require elementary students to take, or history textbooks laden with fragmented factoids, and at the increasing number of standardized tests that all students must pass.

But what does it mean to say that the Basics, in the sense of mastering a set of essential facts, are merely the means of attaining a higher educational purpose? It means that the ultimate goal of being an educated citizen is not the memorizing of information, no matter how important that information may be. Of course, if being an educated citizen was similar to being a successful contestant on TV game shows like "Jeopardy" or "Who Wants to be a Millionaire," then the ability to recall information could indeed be considered a goal. Yet to be a well-informed citizen it is not enough to remember that Pearl Harbor was bombed by the Japanese in 1941 or that the First Amendment of the United States Constitution guarantees our freedom of speech, press, and the right to assemble peacefully. Being an educated citizen implies that one can explain, among other things, why and in what context the Japanese bombed Pearl Harbor, as well as the reasons why the First Amendment is so important for a democratic society. In short, an educated citizen is one who is thoughtful and critical; one who can analyze political ideas and decisions, make connections between the past and the present, and consider issues from multiple perspectives. Since what is at stake here is not a cursory familiarity but a deep and complex understanding of social, historical, political, and economic issues, the ability to recall information can play only a minor role in attaining this goal.

If it is a worthy educational purpose in a democratic society to cultivate citizens who are thoughtful and critical, where does the memorization of information fit in? I would argue that the memorization of facts, dates, words, and formulas must be in the service of this higher educational purpose. That is, the information that we require students to memorize is significant only in relation to the goal of gaining a deeper understanding of a problem in math and science, an event in history, or a novel in English. In themselves these bits of information are meaningless and there is absolutely no justification for requiring students to learn them. To ask students to recall that Pearl Harbor was bombed in 1941 is pointless, unless we can help them understand that it was this bombing that triggered the United States' active involvement in World War II, which was relatively late in the war and came only after it was directly attacked. This fact is significant because it sheds light on the American foreign policy in the twentieth century, one that was motivated much more by self-interest and global domination than by a concern for the suffering of oppressed groups and the denial of human rights abroad.

Similarly, to require elementary school students to memorize numerous lists of spelling words cannot be justified in itself. There is nothing logical or necessary about the way words like *enough* and *weight* are spelled, and English, a language that is not phonetic, has many words whose spelling is entirely arbitrary. The spelling drills that elementary school students engage in would indeed be valuable if they could improve their reading, writing, and thinking skills. However, much of the existing research on spelling raises serious doubts whether such drills actually transfer to other skills. For instance, researchers concluded that "spelling lists of any kind … are limited in their ability to take into account children's prior knowledge of words or to anticipate the specific words that will be greatest use to children in their self-selected writing" (Bekham-Hungler, Williams, Smith, and Dudley-Marling 2003, 306). One is left to conclude that the real reason that teachers send students home with spelling lists is to show parents that their children are learning something tangible, even if it may not be very useful.

I mentioned earlier that the notion of the "basics in education" is often evoked by leaders and ordinary people as an abstraction, without reference to a context that could give it meaning. Clearly, what is basic to the elementary school curriculum is different from that of both the middle and the high school curricula. However, other factors besides the age of the students, such as their social and cultural backgrounds, also play a major role in shaping the Basics of the curriculum. What is basic to a class full of immigrant students is different from a class comprised mainly of children who were born in this country and whose native language is English. As Madeline Grumet argues, the question of the Basics in education should always be posed with reference to people, times, and places (Kincheloe and Steinberg 1995, 16). Otherwise, we risk banishing from the curriculum our students' feelings, imagination, desire, and curiosity — their motivation and enthusiasm to learn.

Moreover, it is precisely our desire to know and to engage in continuous inquiry that, according to Paulo Freire (1994, 53), make us truly human:

> For apart from inquiry, apart from the praxis, individuals cannot be truly human. Knowledge emerges only through invention and re-invention, through the restless, impatient, continuing, hopeful inquiry human beings pursue in the world, with the world, and with each other.

Unfortunately, in many of the current discussions about the Basics in education, knowledge is still regarded by educators and political leaders as merely an object or a thing to be obtained and memorized. In doing so, these people have failed to recognize Freire's insight that knowledge is not a gift or a possession that some individuals have and others lack. On the contrary, knowledge is attained when people come together to exchange ideas, articulate their problems from their own perspectives, and construct meanings that makes sense to them. It is a *process* of inquiry and discovery, an active and restless process that human beings use to make sense of themselves, the world, and the relationships between the two.

FACTS, LIES, AND TEXTBOOKS

Public schools in the United States rely heavily on textbooks to teach students history, English, math, and the sciences. According to A. Graham Down of the Council for Basic Education,

> Textbooks, for better or for worse, dominate what students learn. They set the curriculum, and often the facts learned, in most subjects. For many students, textbooks are their first and sometimes only exposure to books and to reading. The public regards textbooks as authoritative, accurate, and necessary. And teachers rely on them to organize lessons and structure subject matter. (Quoted in Apple 2000, 47-48)

Less well known is the perspective that these textbooks may be bringing about much more harm than good to our students. My own experience, as well as that of other researchers, suggests that rather than creating enthusiasm and stimulating thinking, textbooks usually deaden the minds of students and alienate them from learning. How are textbooks able to accomplish this? They do it, first, by confusing students with a huge list of factoids presented in succession, whose connections are often difficult to discern. Textbooks also mislead students with mis-information and half-truths, removing all ambiguity and complexity from their narrative. And finally, these books bore students to death with their arid, overly detailed, and predictable writing.

History textbooks are a perfect example of this problem. In his monu-mental study of twelve popular history textbooks, James Loewen (1996, 13) concluded that

> the stories that history textbooks tell are predictable; every problem has already been solved or is about to be solved. Textbooks exclude conflict or real suspense. They leave out anything that might reflect badly upon our national charac-ter. When they try for drama, they achieve only melodrama, because readers know that everything will turn out fine in the end.... Most authors of history textbooks don't even try for melodrama. Instead, they write in a tone that if heard aloud might be described as "mumbling lecturer." No wonder stu-dents lose interest.

Loewen goes on to illustrate other problems with history textbooks, such as the fact that they almost never use the past to illuminate the pres-ent or the present to illuminate the past. Also troubling is the fact that most of these books attempt to promote nationalism and blind patriotism as op-posed to independent thinking and a critical historical awareness. Finally, Loewen shows that the history textbooks in his sample are overladen with information, averaging more than 800 pages in length. No student can re-member the hundreds of factoids, main ideas, and key terms contained in these books. "So students and teachers fall back on one main idea: to memorize the terms for the test following each chapter, then forget them to clear the synapses for the next chapter" (Loewen 1996, 14).

What light do these findings about textbooks shed on our discussion of the Basics? First, Loewen's study of history textbooks clearly shows that since the amount of factoids in these books is overwhelming, stu-dents fall into the senseless practice of memorizing the information needed to pass the next test. The problem is not only that most of the in-formation is not retained following the exam, but that the process of learning these numerous, disjointed facts encourages students *not* to think deeply and coherently about history. As a result of the fragmented way in which textbooks present and many teachers teach history, students come away believing that history is merely a list of facts to be learned. In this way, the essence of history, as a furious debate about controversial issues and a struggle between groups of people with opposing interests is lost upon most students. Thus, when new teachers claim that they cannot teach children to think without first giving them some basic information, we need to remind them that it is precisely the emphasis we put on memorizing bits of information that is likely to impede them from thinking critically and coherently.

In addition, when teachers argue that they cannot teach their students to think without first providing them the Basics, they mean that there is a set of facts that constitute the foundation of a particular discipline upon which everything else must rest. Learning the foundational facts in math, history, science, and English is believed to be the key to understanding the more difficult concepts of each of these disciplines. The problem with this argument, as in the case of history, is that learning a set of essential facts does not typically translate into understanding and knowledge. Such learning is similar to getting a picture of the trees but no sense of the entire forest. Genuine learning, understanding, and knowledge, on the other hand, presuppose that one can make connections between various ideas, facts, and events — and not just remember them in isolation. In history and the sciences such connections are often referred to as cause and effect relationships, and without getting a solid grasp of these relationships one cannot claim to know these disciplines.

The argument that there is a set of essential facts and ideas that constitute the foundation of a discipline is also problematic because it assumes that these facts and ideas are indisputable and agreed upon by everybody. While in history and the social sciences it is fairly evident that there are competing interpretations of historical events or psychological development, the existence of divergent theories in the natural sciences that attempt to explain the same phenomenon is much less obvious. When discussing the natural sciences, students of education will often refer to these disciplines as clear-cut and unambiguous. Yet, as I suggested in Chapter Two, every theory, including those in biology, physics, and chemistry is not indisputable but rather one among many possible ways of explaining a given phenomenon. In biology, for instance, Social Darwinism and Creationism are two opposing theories that compete with each other and with more current theories in order to provide a convincing account of the origin and evolution of the human species. The attempts made by a number of school districts around the country to ban the teaching of Social Darwinism in biology classes should be viewed as an effort to strip this subject of its core: the heated debate about the origin and nature of the living world.

Many of the discussions about the Basics in education are misleading in that they attempt to oversimplify issues that are far more multifaceted and complex. Christopher Columbus, for example, is presented in many textbooks as the brave hero who discovered the New World. Little is mentioned in these books about the fact that Columbus was not really the first European to reach America nor about the rampage and destruction that he and those who followed him inflicted on the indigenous population they encountered. In fact, Loewen shows that the traditional account of Columbus presented in many history textbooks is full of omissions, half-truths, and lies, thus making it virtually impossible for students to gain a clear understanding of the conquest of the Americas. Such an understanding can only come about if textbooks and teachers cease to portray an overly simplistic, vanilla version of history that often leads students to a mindless endorsement of the people in power. Loewen's (1996, 70) alternative to this feel-good history calls for viewing Columbus from at least two diverse perspectives:

> Columbus's conquest of Haiti can be seen as an amazing feat of courage and imagination by the first of many empire builders. It can also be understood as a bloody atrocity that left a legacy of genocide and slavery that endures in some degree to this day. Both views of Columbus are valid; indeed, Columbus's importance in history owes precisely to his being both a heroic navigator *and* a great plunderer.

BASIC FACTS, BASIC CHOICES

Loewen's depiction of Columbus as both a heroic navigator and a great plunderer calls our attention to the fact that knowledge is never neutral and that it is always informed by a particular ideological vantage point. This means that what gets designated as knowledge cannot simply be regarded as "objective" truths or "impartial" facts. For instance, the answer to the question of whether George W. Bush or Al Gore actually won the 2000 presidential elections will depend on one's political perspective and on the way in which one interprets the historical record. In short, what we consider reality and knowledge is never value-free; it is always shaped by our interests, desires, and beliefs about ourselves and the world.

The concept that knowledge is never value-free implies also that reality is not naturally preordained, inevitable, or unchangeable. Indeed, many things that were considered common knowledge in previous generations are regarded as inaccuracies or even outright errors today. The fact that our conception of the world is constantly changing suggests further that knowledge is socially constructed, meaning that reality is always shaped by the social conventions, values, and practices of a particular historical and cultural context. Since in almost all cases it is the dominant class that controls the media, advertising companies, book publishers, and other information producers, it, in effect, is able to determine what is considered knowledge. An obvious example is the mainstream media in the United States, much of which is controlled by a handful of corporations and very wealthy individuals. Since the vast majority of news in this country is produced by a few media giants, it is they who ultimately control people's knowledge of both domestic and international affairs. And since the livelihood of the media corporations is dependent on the advertisement contracts they obtain, they rarely report news that would offend their advertisers.

All of this is not new and, in fact, in the past few decades much has been written about the relation of knowledge, power, and education.[2] However, one aspect of this conversation that is particularly pertinent to our discussion of the Basics is the question of "*Whose* knowledge is of most worth?" This question reminds us that when we claim that students need to know the Basics, we need to be prepared to explain why some facts, ideas, or texts are more important than others. Why is it more important for high school students to read Mark Twain or Nathaniel Hawthorne and not Zora Neale Hurston or Alice Walker? Although in the past few years some effort has been made to include more minority authors in the curriculum, there is still a significant imbalance between the attention given to white versus minority writers. Thus, the school curriculum — and by extension what has been called official knowledge — always represents a selective tradition: A particular choice of what constitutes legitimate knowledge usually legitimizes the dominant group's perspective while disenfranchizing that of subordinate groups (Apple 2000, 46).

Moreover, as Madeline Grumet (1995, 15) eloquently writes, the very word *Basic* compels a specific selection:

> It demands the discrimination that ranks some issues as essential and others as not. Here is the BASIC thing to remember, we say, wielding the giant spotlight of our attention, and suddenly all else falls into darkness. I, myself, have always been pretty suspicious of that spotlight, always straining to see what lives in its shadow, always hoping that whoever directs its beam will be distracted and turn too quickly, letting the light pour into the world we weren't supposed to see.

Grumet reminds us that there is something not only limiting but also arbitrary about the term Basic. It is limiting in that the curriculum directs our attention to particular questions and themes, thereby suppressing or concealing others. And it is arbitrary because, as noted above, the curriculum determines that some issues are essential while others are not, without really providing a convincing rationale for this selection.

Does it follow that we should just drop the notion of the Basics from all discussions about the purpose of education and the content of the curriculum? My fear is that simply abandoning this concept will not do the trick because it can be easily replaced by an equally problematic term. What seems to be fairly obvious is that the way of conceptualizing the Basics, as a set of essential texts, facts, and formulas, is no longer tenable. Instead of viewing the Basics as a list of facts to remember, we need, following Grumet, to begin thinking about them in terms of relationships; namely, the various relations between the students and the world. And rather than talking about the curriculum as a body of information, we would be better served if we considered it as a conversation, as a process of making sense with our students of the world that surrounds us.

The advantages of viewing the Basics in terms of the relations between people and the world as opposed to a list of things to remember are many. First, such a conception of the Basics enables us to understand what is unique to education, a process of introducing people to ways of being in the world that are new to them and making connections between their existing experiences and this new world. Unlike both training and indoctrination, what is essential in education is not so much the acquisition of new information or skills, but the way in which the learner interprets and interacts with this new knowledge. Second, such a conception of the Basics will help to alleviate one of the most serious problems in education today: the fact that so many students are not motivated to learn and consider school boring or a waste of time. Since this alternative conception of the Basics puts a premium on the vital connections between learner and learned, it is reasonable to assume that many students who currently feel alienated from their schools will become much more engaged in the learning process.

A conception of the Basics that stresses the vital relations between the students and the world will result not only in more engaged and meaningful learning but also in learning that is deeper and more critical. Because the emphasis is no longer on recalling information but on making connections between this information, the students' existing knowledge, and broader social issues, students gain an understanding of the subject that goes far beyond the superficial rote learning of traditional education. Ultimately, this alternative conception of the Basics and the learning that it supports can work to reverse the erosion of democracy and critical citizenry in the United States mentioned at the beginning of this chapter. Such learning will foster citizens who are not only well informed but also reflective about themselves, their community, and the relationship between the two and the larger society.

TEACHING THE BASICS

Assuming that we agree that what is essential in education is not the acquisition of new information or skills but the way in which the learner interprets and interacts with this new knowledge, how should we go about teaching the Basics? Clearly, the traditional models of teaching and learning, based on rote learning and memorization, have not helped students get excited about learning in general or about different topics in depth. Indeed, such models have historically led many students to hate subjects such as math, history, or English and, to feel alienated from learning and their schools. In light of this sad state of affairs, Eric Cooper (1989, 105) concludes that

> there is an obvious need in this country to move beyond instruction that limits students' academic experiences to the use of poorly developed materials, that engages them in seatwork that may be improperly designed for their academic needs, or that forces them to attend to a series of activities geared to elicit the simple regurgitation of facts and figures.

Yet even if we assume that the materials we are using are excellent and that the students are actively engaged in the learning process, we still need to explain how to teach students the basic skills (such as research skills) they need to become independent and reflective thinkers. According to David Kobrin (1995, 506), traditional models for teaching skills usually advise you to work sequentially, beginning with the Basics and then moving on to more complex combinations. These teaching models assume that the development of good research skills and attitudes can be separated from the tasks the students are working on. However, Kobrin's experience of collaborating with teachers from public high schools in Providence, Rhode Island, on a project designed to help kids become student historians, led him to identify some problems with this approach. He argues (1995, 506) correctly that

> the skills needed to do a project are also intricate parts of doing the project. In our experience, skills were best learned while struggling with the project. In other words, we came to see the development of skills as part of the project, rather than preparation for it. We did not make a clear separation between working as a student historian, and learning how to work as a student historian.

Kobrin's conclusions are supported by various educational theorists. Vygotsky (1978, 83), for example, asserts that "the mind is not a complex network of general capabilities such as observation, attention, memory, judgment, and so forth, but a set of specific capabilities, each of which is, to some extent, independent of the others and is developed independently." The implication of this assertion is that learning is not really the acquisition of the ability to think in general; it is the acquisition of many specialized abilities of thinking about a variety of things in different contexts. Hence when teaching students basic skills we should always make sure that these skills are an integral part of a particular task we are asking students to do that makes sense to them. Following Kobrin's and Vygotsky's insights, we should not expect that students will be able to transfer skills they learned working on a specific project to a different set of tasks and circumstances.

Yet even when we attempt to teach students basic skills as part of a particular projec, as Kobrin recommends, there is another discussion that needs to be considered. Indeed, Kobrin's experience confirms one of the first lessons that all new teachers learn when they begin their careers and what educators like John Dewey insisted on more than a hundred years ago: You need to begin your lesson not with *skills* but with the *student*. Kobrin's experience as well as my own suggest that unless students perceive reasons of their own to care about the particular topic that is being taught, they will lack the energy and commitment needed to learn the skills and concepts required to understand it. In Kobrin's words (1995, 508):

> When it comes to motivation and involvement for student historian projects we found that the teacher's energy alone was never enough. Since it was the kids who needed to be involved actively, raising basic questions, defining answers, creating understandings, there were limits to what a teacher could do. The students needed to go through a process that helped them develop reasons of their own.

Insofar as good teaching requires us to begin with the students — that is, with arousing their interest to want to learn about the topic — teaching the Basics of a subject is no different than teaching the more complex ideas, concepts, or formulas. Seasoned teachers know that there are numerous and varied ways to arouse students' excitement about a subject and have probably developed a repertoire of methods and techniques to achieve this goal. Identifying such methods and techniques is not the purpose here and, in fact, a great many books and articles have already been written that address this topic. Rather, my aim is to outline the *process* of teaching students the basic skills needed to be a researcher of history so that teachers in other disciplines can adapt this approach to meet their individual goals and needs.

How should history and social studies teachers proceed to teach basic research skills once the students' interest in and commitment to learning about the topic has been established? Kobrin's experience with public high school students in Providence suggests that it is crucial to limit the amount of basic rules we ask students to learn and to keep them simple. Limiting the amount of basic rules and concepts that students need to learn is important because the goal is not to give students an exhaustive list of techniques and tricks they can use to solve all the problems historians face. The aim is rather to provide students with guidelines that will help them figure out solutions to problems, including those never encountered before. Since the aim is not the memorization of rules but the ability to use these rules to solve new problems, it is also important to keep the basic rules simple so that students really comprehend them and know how to use them correctly. Ultimately, the simple rules approach is very successful in teaching students basic skills because it fosters independent thinkers and learners.

> I like to think of the simplified rules for historians, at their best, as a teacher within each student. When building complex skills from simple rules it was the student who was telling the student how to proceed. The teacher acted as mentor and advisor to the neophyte. Once students got to the level where they were using the building block rules regularly — almost "automatically" — the students used the guidelines virtually to teach themselves. (Kobrin 1995, 508)

My own experience of working with teacher candidates for many years supports this finding. When my students conduct group presentations at the end of each semester, invariably the groups that are able to limit the amount of information they present and keep their lesson simple make the most effective presentations. On the other hand, those presentations in which students attempt to get across too much information almost always end up being not only confusing but also unexciting for the other students in the class. The message that I try to get across to my students is that *less is more* — that it is far better to teach people a few basic ideas in depth than to try to cover a great deal of information in a superficial manner, information that the students will neither remember nor have any use for in the future.

The final issue that teachers need to take into account when attempting to teach their students basic skills is that in order to get all students to learn these skills it is vital to get them to collaborate with each other. In particular, students from diverse backgrounds and with different learning styles and perspectives can assist each other in learning basic research skills and concepts, a task that would be difficult for some of them when working independently. Kobrin's experience (1995, 510) with high school students indicates that

> complex analytic tasks that might have been too much for a student when working individually could be tackled more easily when several students contributed what they knew, what they felt, and how they thought. Gender differences, racial perspectives, first languages other than English, recent

immigrant and native-born experiences, even social and economic class gaps all became tools that kids could use to un-
ravel the complicated human stories hidden in documents
and primary sources — as long as the students willingly de-
pended on one another.

My own work with teacher candidates confirms Kobrin's insight. I
have witnessed over and over that when students work in groups on
various tasks and projects, the diversity of student experiences greatly
enhances their understanding of complex concepts and skills. Working
in groups, students are able to construct knowledge through a process of
sharing their opinions with the group and revising these opinions in
light of other people's views, experiences, and values. Through interacting among themselves, students gain a deeper awareness of concepts
such as hermeneutics, qualitative research, and constructivism. They
draw on their own experiences in order to give examples of such complex concepts, thereby demonstrating not only that they comprehend
them but also that knowledge is a social construction and not something
that only "experts" possess.

CONCLUSION

Although the examples given in this chapter to explain the significance of the Basics and how to teach them are taken mostly from the
field of history, the conclusions reached are valid for other subjects as
well. The notion that what is basic to education is not the acquisition of
new information or skills but the way in which the learner interprets
this new knowledge is true not only for history but also for subjects
such as Science, English and Math. Memorizing basic laws and formulas in Chemistry or Geometry, for instance, is senseless unless one can
understand how to use them to solve new problems. Such an understanding assumes that a person has grasped the significance of a particular law or formula and can determine in what context it can be
applied. Moreover, knowledge of a scientific theory entails much more
than merely learning the facts that make up this theory. Just as genuine
historical awareness means that one is able to explain the connection
between various events in the past and present, true scientific knowledge implies that one is familiar with the relationships between the individual facts that make up a theory.

Finally, the process I have outlined above for teaching students the basic skills needed to be a researcher of History is, I believe, equally applicable to Math, English and the Sciences. Principles such as teaching students basic skills as part of a project, beginning the lesson with the students' experiences, teaching basic skills through the use of simple rules, and getting students to collaborate with each other, are all sound pedagogy in other subjects too. For example, teaching students writing skills is now widely recognized in English as significant only in a context that is relevant and makes sense to them. Independent writing drills that are not part of a meaningful project are discouraged today in part because students view them as tedious and mind-numbing. Likewise, teaching students basic research skills through the use of simple rules is an approach that is valuable not only in History but also in the natural sciences where scientists rely heavily on research skills. Rules such as comparing their results to those of other students are excellent tools that can help students working in a lab become more reflective, make logical inferences, and solve problems as they arise. The lesson to learn here is that though the questions, ideas, and methods of inquiry vary from discipline to discipline, the most fruitful way to teach students basics skills and concepts in each subject remains relatively the same.

NOTES

1. See her essay in Kincheloe and Steinberg (1995, 19).
2. Quoted in Michael W. Apple (2000, 47-48).
3. See, for instance, Michael W. Apple (1979; 1996; 2000) and Kincheloe, Steinberg, and Villaverde (1999).

Chapter Four

Keeping Students Busy Enhances Learning

Conventional wisdom says that teachers need to keep students busy. Good teachers, it is believed, are those who are able to control their classes and whose students spend all or most of their time on task. "Classroom management" has been one of the most popular buzz words in the last decade and is considered preferable by many educators to "discipline," a word that suggests the need to control and keep people in line. Actually, classroom management maintains some of the same overtones as its predecessor: students need to be managed and controlled. Moreover, few people have noted that management is a term borrowed from business and that the implication is that the same concepts and practices that are used there can easily be applied to education. The popularity of this term is indicative of the general state of schooling in the United States in which the connections between business and education are steadily growing and the models that have worked in business are increasingly used to evaluate education. Thus, concepts such as efficiency, productivity, results-orientation, and gains have been introduced to the discourse of schooling, without much attention to the fact that we are dealing with children, not profits, and with cultivating moral and critical human beings rather than buying and selling.

Also neglected are the implications of some of the common practices that teachers use in their classrooms to manage students as well as some problematic assumptions about the nature of children, knowledge, and the social context that are at the basis of many management models.

These mistaken assumptions lead many teachers and schools to prize silence over excitement, obedience over critical thinking, and rote learning over creativity. In what follows, I take a hard look at a number of practices used to control students and the erroneous beliefs that inform such practices. I also show how these misguided assumptions lead to the false conclusion that such practices are worthy, if not essential, educational tools. Beginning with an alternative set of premises about children, knowledge, and the social context can pave the way not only to different but also to more humane pedagogical insights and classroom management practices.

Do-Nows: A Novel Management Tool

One such practice that is very popular in many areas, but often unnoticed, is the use of "do-now" assignments at the beginning of lessons. Sometimes referred to as The Problem of the Day, do-nows are relatively short assignments that usually consist of a couple of questions or problems given to students as soon as they enter the classroom. The questions given to students are intended to serve as a review of something that was covered earlier or to get students to think about the topic of the day. Typically, these assignments take about five minutes to complete which allows the teacher to take attendance and engage in other administrative duties while the students are settling down and working on the questions. Most of my in-service teacher-candidate students were very enthusiastic about this relatively new instructional technique, often noting that "It works great for me," and "It gets those bouncy students to begin working right away and not goof off."

Currently, a large percentage of middle and secondary schools and a growing number of elementary schools across the nation expect teachers to begin their lessons with a do-now assignment much like they expect them to write the aim of the lesson on the blackboard when the period begins. To be sure, I am not opposed to the use of do-now assignments per se, and I can definitely see the educational value of getting students to settle down and work on a question related to the topic of the day or something they have already learned *in order to get them thinking*. The problem is that the do-nows are typically used in such a routine and standardized manner that they defeat the purpose of getting students to think. Further, the over-use of this pedagogical technique diminishes much of the spontaneity of the initial encounter between the teacher and students.

Imagine, if you will, what it is like to be a thirteen-year-old student, having to take six to seven classes every day that all begin with a do-now exercise. In some cases, the teacher does not even greet the student but simply motions him or her to sit down and begin working on the do-now questions on the board. It is not too difficult to see that after a while such exercises may become tiresome and dull for the student and he or she gets accustomed to just going through the motions with these assignments. Indeed, I have observed many students doing just that when they are greeted at the door with a do-now question, not to mention those who simply do not bother to do the assignment. In short, for many students the do-now assignments at the beginning of each lesson have turned into yet another classroom ritual, whose educational value they cannot understand.

Unfortunately, I suspect that these students are probably right and that in many cases these assignments are devoid of any genuine educational purpose. That is, the unstated reason that many teachers like to assign a do-now exercise at the start of each lesson is that it gives them a relatively easy way to gain control of their classes during those first moments when students are typically very active, moving about, and conversing with their friends. In effect, this assignment is a useful management tool that forces students to sit down and begin working on a problem right away rather than playing, bouncing around, or just relaxing.

Given the fact that the do-now exercises are frequently used as a management tool whose educational purpose is highly questionable, it should not come as a big surprise that many students resent and even rebel against this instrument of control. One implication from this observation is that teachers should always keep in mind the importance of breaking from normal routines and tedious rituals in order to keep students interested and engaged in learning. "What would happen," I used to ask my in-service teacher candidates who raved about this instructional tool, "if instead of beginning each lesson with a do-now, you occasionally start by getting the students to sit in a circle and talk about something meaningful to them?" The common reply I received was that "our students will take advantage of this situation, continue talking and not pay attention." Such a response confirms my assumption that many new and seasoned teachers are more concerned with gaining control of their students than with establishing meaningful relations or doing something different and creative with them.

Yet in saying that many new and veteran teachers are overly concerned with controlling their students and managing their classes, I do not mean to suggest that the teachers themselves are to blame for this state of affairs. Clearly, there are tremendous pressures placed on teachers, especially new ones, to demonstrate that they can manage their classes, get students to work, and prepare them to take the standardized tests. I have heard of teachers who were reprimanded by their principal if he or she walked into their classroom and the aim and do-now assignment were not written on the blackboard. Combine this with the fact that middle and secondary teachers are often assigned six to seven classes a day, with three minutes between each period and fifteen minutes for lunch, and you can easily see why many teachers welcome this management tool.

Moreover, school principals, much like teachers, come under enormous pressures by administrators and boards of education to make sure that theirs students are meeting state and national standards. Hence the fact that many educators are overly concerned with maintaining control and managing their classes should be viewed as a systemic educational problem in this country rather than one that pertains to individual teachers or principals. In an educational system that values efficiency, productivity, and standardization above all else, the use of do-now assignments as yet another management tool makes sense.

A key issue that needs to be considered regarding the widespread use of do-now assignments are the consequences that this practice has both for students and teachers. It has already been mentioned that the routinization of this exercise, like the ringing of the school bell, seems to diminish much of the spontaneity of the initial encounter between teacher and students. Yet, as Martin Buber suggests, a meaningful encounter between teachers and their students is crucial to establish a deep relationship between them and to arouse students' interest to learn something new.[1] My own experience of observing the routine use of do-now exercises indicates that it undermines both the quality of the relationship between the teacher and the students and students' desire to learn. The message that students get when they walk into a class and are immediately instructed to get working on an assignment is that school is a place that values busywork more than interaction, and obedience to authority more than freedom and choice.

No Recess and Increased Time on Task

Another phenomenon that limits the opportunities for social interaction is the diminished role that recess plays in many schools. Tom Jambor, who has studied this issue for years argues that

> recess, once a reliable part of American children's school life, now is absent or only an afterthought in many schools. As a result, opportunities for social interchange are minimal. All too many schools now greatly restrict talking among children before class, during class, during lunch, and when standing in line to go anywhere. Indeed, recess may be the *only* time when children can interact without adult intervention or restriction. This makes school recess more vital than ever to social development. (Jambor 1994, 18)

The diminished role that recess plays in the life of many schools is all the more surprising if we consider that it is a basic human need. Recess can be defined as a break from what we are engaged in or a period of time away from the task at hand (Jambor 1994, 17). Such breaks are common in court proceedings, congressional sessions, and in the regular course of the day of any office worker. Jambor points out correctly that recess is not only necessary but useful for all adults: "It helps us get through the workday; to reduce fatigue and burnout; to enhance on-task behavior, enthusiasm and energy; and to develop a more positive outlook on our work" (Jambor 1994, 17).

If we acknowledge that recess is a basic necessity for adults, there can be no doubt that children have, at the very least, similar needs. Children are natural movers, doers, and socializers, and forcing them to engage in prolonged periods of seatwork will obviously lead them to fatigue and restlessness. Moreover, as Pellegrini (1991, 40) has noted, "children need recess because they are temporarily bored with the immediate classroom environment" (Pellegrini 1991, 40). Yet even though these ideas are not new and there is ample theoretical and empirical evidence to support these claims, we still confine elementary children to their desks for prolonged periods of monotonous work that would tax many adults.

In addition, as Jambor and other researchers have recognized, recess can have a significant impact on the social development of children. This is because it gives students an opportunity to acquire various social skills such as cooperation, compromising, negotiating roles, and problem solving. Interactive games such as Tag and Hide and Seek enable children to practice compromising and negotiating roles with each other, without which the games cannot take place. Pellegrini and Glickman (1989, 24) sum up this point well when they write that

> recess is one of the few times during the school day when children are free to exhibit a wide range of social competencies — sharing, cooperation, negative and passive language — in the context that they see meaningful. Only at recess does the playground become one of the few places where children can actually define and enforce meaningful social interaction during the day. Without recess, the children lose an important educational experience.

In fact, research has shown that play and recess activities can enhance not only the social development of children but also their cognitive, emotional, and moral development. This research indicates that children playing during recess may be practicing various cognitive skills, such as problem solving, that they later transfer to the work in the classroom (Pellegrini and Glickman 1989, 24). Likewise, when children negotiate, compromise, and cooperate while playing games during recess, they are gaining insight on the importance of considering the feelings of others and viewing events from multiple perspectives. Such insights are essential for children to learn so that they can develop into mature adults as well as reflective and caring citizens in a democratic society.

If recess is indeed so valuable to the social, cognitive, and moral development of children and is one of the only times when they can interact freely with each other, why is it being restricted or even eliminated in many school districts? In New Haven, for instance, recess is not part of the formal curriculum for public elementary schools, though a teacher can use her discretion and opt to take her class outside to get a break if the children seem tired or restless. Of course, we would never allow teachers to use their discretion about whether students should learn reading or math every day. According to Jambor (1994, 19), the problem is that

> too many adults who influence early childhood curricula and school schedules do not understand the value and importance of recess as a time to play. Many teachers, administrators, and parents consider recess wasted time. They believe that recess is, at best, peripheral to children's learning experi-

ences and that children learn best in school when they focus on basic skills and stay on task.

In an educational climate in which there is a growing emphasis on testing children and on teaching the Basics (as if play is not basic), recess is viewed as a distraction from the content and the rigor of the academic curriculum that needs to be covered. As Jambor (1994, 19) notes, "education policymakers are so obsessed with academic attainment that they have eliminated or drastically reduced other activities which are important in children's total growth, development, and learning." Thus, subjects such as art and music are usually the first to be cut from the curriculum because they are considered extras that do not contribute to the academic achievement of children. Yet in putting so much emphasis on cognitive achievement and on-task behavior, we run the risk of stifling children's other developmental domains, including their social, emotional, and moral development.

Moreover, since one of the arguments against recess is that it wastes time and takes away from the precious moments to engage in on-task assignments, it seems only natural to closely examine what tasks children are being pulled away from. As Alfie Kohn has shown in his book *Beyond Discipline* (1996), the field of classroom management has been almost completely oblivious to the question of what we are asking students to do and how that is contributing to their lack of motivation to engage in various tasks. Kohn's research (1996, 20) reveals that, in most cases, on-task time refers to engaging in "individual seatwork involving reading textbooks, completing worksheets and quizzes, and answering questions such as 'Who can tell me what the square root of 16 is?'" Many students have a hard time getting excited about these tasks, to say the least, because they tend to be tedious and boring and prevent them from interacting with each other. They sense that these assignments have little educational value and that teachers use them routinely in order to better manage students' behavior.

What message are students supposed to get from regularly engaging in on-task exercises like the ones described above? One obvious message is that learning has nothing to do with choosing something to explore in depth or getting excited about the activity that one is doing. On the contrary, learning is essentially about following the teacher's prescriptions and completing the work that was assigned. In recess, on the other hand, children learn that social interaction is not only fun but also meaningful and that through play they can gain a deeper awareness of themselves and their relationships to others. Perhaps one of the reasons why many educators currently consider recess a distraction or a waste of time is that the lessons that children learn at recess while playing are almost the exact opposite of the lessons that are taught when they are engaged in on-task behavior. Unlike recess in which kids have an opportunity to freely explore themselves and the world around them, in class they are expected primarily to listen and digest the ideas and rules of others.

Of course, the answer to the question whether or not an activity is a waste of time is always relative to the educational goal one is trying to achieve. If our aim is that children develop socially and cognitively, then giving them recess is a good idea since, as most of the research suggests, it can greatly enhance this goal. Conversely, one can probably make a pretty strong case that many of the so-called "on-task" exercises that teachers assign are worthless because they do little to promote student learning and cognitive development. Completing worksheets and individual seatwork typically result in students merely regurgitating the information that is presented to them and do not help them construct meanings and reach genuine understandings. Much like the spelling lists given to students to memorize, using worksheets is a tangible assignment whose educational value is highly questionable. And like the do-now exercises discussed above, they help the teacher manage the class and maintain control as the students are kept busy doing something, albeit something that they did not choose and may have little interest in doing.

SOME PROBLEMATIC ASSUMPTIONS

Every theory of classroom management is based on a set of assumptions about the nature of children, knowledge, and the social context. Even veteran teachers who are skilled at running their classes and claim that they have learned their craft from experience are buying into various assumptions about children, learning, and the relations between teachers and students. But despite their growing popularity, classroom management theories rarely make visible the basic premises they are grounded on. Exposing these assumptions is crucial because they "color everything that happens in classrooms, from the texts that are assigned to the texture of casual interactions with students" (Kohn 1996, 1). Kohn correctly points out that precisely because they have such a significant

impact on every aspect of education, it is necessary to expose these beliefs and determine whether or not they can survive careful scrutiny.

THE NATURE OF CHILDREN

One set of beliefs that needs to be closely examined concerns the nature of children and by extension all people. Kohn's comprehensive
study of both traditional and more modern classroom management theories suggests that almost all of them accept the premise that students
must be closely regulated if they are to do anything productive. He emphasizes that these theories do not simply advocate having some reasonable structure in schools but insist that external control is necessary for
without it children are unlikely to learn and behave properly. This view
is exemplified by a theory called *Assertive Discipline* whose authors claim
that "children are not innately motivated to behave in school" (Canter
and Canter 1992, 7). Most of the theories that Kohn surveyed share the
belief that "children need to be told exactly what the adult expects of
them, as well as what will happen if they don't do what they're told"
(Kohn 1996, 2). The underlying assumption is, therefore, that children
are inherently mischievous and noncompliant and cannot be trusted to
regulate themselves.

To illustrate how this assumption impacts classroom practice let's re-
consider the reasons why the use of do-nows and time on-task have become the norm in so many schools. As stated above, these techniques are
popular because they get students to work on a concrete assignment as
soon as they enter the class and help maintain order in the classroom.
Teachers who use these practices claim that their students will not do the
work unless they are given very specific instructions and threatened with
consequences if they do not comply. Hence the assumptions that students
cannot be trusted to regulate themselves and that they need to be tightly
controlled in order to be productive lead directly to the conclusion that we
need practices such as do-nows and increased time on-task to manage
their behavior. Yet this conclusion is plausible only if one buys into their
underlying assumptions about the nature of children. In contrast, if one
begins with the assumption that children are inherently trustworthy and
good or even with the more likely premise that humans are capable of
generosity just as much as selfishness, one will necessarily arrive at very
different conclusions about how to maintain order in the classroom.

The latter premise, according to Kohn, is supported by numerous
studies in developmental and social psychology. These studies suggest

that even children as young as two years old have the capacity to respond with generosity and empathy towards others. When children do
not act in a way that is consistent with these capacities, they "may be un-
aware of the effects of their actions on others, or unable to act otherwise"
(Kohn 1996, 9). Older children may feel pressured by the situation to act
unkindly or they may have learned to rely on power and aggression
rather than compassion because this is what they have witnessed adults
do. In any case, the point is that children are not born selfish or aggres-
sive and when they do act in destructive ways, we need to look carefully
at the various factors that are contributing to the problematic behavior.

What might a classroom in which the teacher subscribes to the view
that children are capable of reflection, generosity, and compassion look
like? The following vignette from an elementary classroom provides a
good example of this approach and of a constructivist approach to learning and management.

> The students in this active second-grade classroom are work-
> ing at four learning centers scattered around the room. At the
> writing center, four students are writing about butterflies
> they had seen earlier in the day. There are only places at the
> writing center for four students at one time and two addi-
> tional students want to enter the center. The two students
> look at a board near the writing center and see all the "tickets"
> have been taken. They also see that two students have an-
> other ten minutes on the timer left at the center. They write
> their names on the small notebook size chalkboard that holds
> a place for them, and they go to the Reading Bookshelf and
> begin reading books they had started the previous day.
> (Freiberg 1999, 14)

One of the first things we notice in this example is that the children
are active and are able to move about; they are not forced to sit at their
desks for extended periods of time. The fact that the children are active is significant because it means that the teacher is taking into account their need to be movers and doers, much like teachers who
make sure that their students get enough breaks. More importantly,
being active implies that the students are excited about learning and
that they are getting much more out of the activities compared to
those who are passive or bored. The fact that the children are actively
involved in the learning centers suggests further that the teacher has

attended carefully to the tasks that are available for them to engage in. By providing students with meaningful and exciting tasks, the teacher has helped them stay focused, thereby avoiding or minimizing discipline problems.

Second, the students in this class can make choices about the type of activity they want to do and what they want to learn for portions of the day. Although there is a structure in place in this classroom, the students have some freedom of choice within this structure and, like the two students who wanted to go to the writing center, are able to gain practice in making decisions and managing their time. Finally, because the students work in groups in each of the learning centers, they enjoy the opportunity to interact with each other, exchange ideas, and work together. This interaction, as theorists like Dewey and Vygotsky have shown, promotes children's cognitive, social, and moral development. While a classroom like this second grade is not one in which one can hear a needle drop, by communicating and working together the children are helping each other keep the structure intact. In effect, they are regulating each other while the teacher serves as a guide or facilitator to help address questions and problems as they arise. Because students' basic needs are taken into account, such an approach to discipline is much stronger and more humane than the traditional model that relies on external control and consequences imposed on students who misbehave.

THE NATURE OF KNOWLEDGE

Besides the beliefs about the nature of children, classroom management theories are also grounded on a set of assumptions about the nature of knowledge. Kohn (1996, 20) argues that "programs of classroom management rarely betray any awareness of, much less commitment to, the sort of learning that could be called constructivist or learner-centered." Instead, they rest on a traditional model of learning in which knowledge is viewed as a set of facts, dates, names, and information that the teacher transmits to the students. Paulo Freire calls this model of learning the "banking concept of education" and claims that it is based on a conception of knowledge as a motionless, static, and predictable reality. Unlike the constructivist approach in which knowledge is considered something that the students create or interpret, thereby making it meaningful to themselves, in banking education to know is to learn those facts that have already been discovered by others. In the banking concept, education becomes

> an act of depositing, in which the students are the deposito-
> ries and the teacher is the depositor. Instead of communicat-
> ing, the teacher issues communiqués and makes deposits
> which the students patiently receive, memorize and repeat.
> (Freire 1994, 53)

Based on this traditional notion of knowledge, curricula are designed, activities created, and homework is assigned to promote student learning. Schools that mandate the use of do-now exercises and time on-task embrace this conception of knowledge since, in most cases, the assignments given to students consist of answering questions in textbooks or doing low-level worksheets. All too often, teachers do not bother to get their students' input on the tasks that are assigned to them. Classroom management models are then invented to ensure that students function effectively in this tedious and unexciting learning environment. These models, as Kohn has shown, typically rely on some sort of reward and punishment system in order to get students to comply. Yet the implementation of such management models makes sense only if one initially accepts the notion of knowledge that they rest on. If, on the other hand, we posit an alternative conception of knowledge, we can expect to arrive at a very different approach to classroom management.

Consider, if you will, a conception of knowledge not as a thing or an object, but rather sharing that arises out of interaction and dialogue. In this view, knowledge is not a possession, a gift, or a commodity that some people have and some people don't. Rather it is something that is *constructed* when an individual interacts with others or a text in order to exchange ideas and interpret the world. Thus when a teacher conducts a discussion with her class on a topic of interest, the teacher and students are engaging in the process of producing knowledge and creating meaning. The topic of interest may be a current event that was covered in the news recently, a problem in science, or a story that the class has read. But in each case, to really understand and *know* the event, problem, or story, it is not enough to memorize the various facts and details that it includes. Rather, genuine knowledge means that an individual can interpret and makes sense of the relationships between the various facts and details of a particular topic.

What can this alternative conception of knowledge teach us about classroom management? One obvious implication is that teachers need to promote rather than discourage opportunities for interaction, dialogue, and collaboration among students. As Kohn (1996, 74) puts it, "the wrestling with dilemmas, the clash of ideas, the need to take others' needs into account — these are ultimately more meaningful than any list of rules or guidelines that may ultimately result." Out of such a debate and clash of ideas, the students could create rules that maintain a certain structure and order in the classroom. However, the *process* of engaging in deep conversation to create these rules is just as important as the product, the rules themselves that were invented. Moreover, since conversation and interaction among students is valued, the use of management techniques aimed at controlling the students and keeping them busy and docile, like do-nows and individual seatwork, will no longer be prized. Engaging in group work or class discussions, on the other hand, would then be considered not only as time on-task but as a way of allowing students to practice regulating themselves.

THE SOCIAL CONTEXT

The last set of assumptions I wish to consider that are at the basis of all classroom management theories concerns the nature of the social context. By the nature of the social context, I mean the character and quality of the relations between teachers and students, as well as among students themselves. Many, if not most, management theories put the adult in the position of the creator and enforcer of rules and the imposer of unpleasant consequences for children who break the rules. The problem, according to Kohn, is that such a position undermines the caring alliance between teachers and students, so crucial for children's development. Kohn illustrates this point when he writes (1996, 27) that

> to help an impulsive, aggressive, or insensitive student become more responsible, we have to gain more insight into why she is acting that way. That, in turn, is more likely to happen when the student feels close enough to us (and safe enough with us) to explain how things look from her point of view. The more students see us as punishers, the less likely it is that we can create the sort of environment where things can change.

My own experience of listening to scores of new teachers describe their difficulties with various disruptive students confirms this point. Once a teacher takes on the role of the enforcer of rules and punishment, it is very difficult for him or her to gain a real understanding of the causes of the unruly behavior and to get the student to make any changes.

Conversely, if teachers interact with their students as caring human beings rather than as enforcers of rules and punishment, the nature of the relationship between teachers and students changes completely. One does not have to be an expert in psychology or human relations to understand that students are more likely to be respectful when teachers, and adults in general, show that they respect them. Tom Jambor (1994, 17) recalls how he viewed his elementary teachers during recess:

> I enjoyed my teachers in that informal context. They were different there. They seemed just like regular people. They laughed at our silly jokes and behavior, they hugged us in joy or after a bump or bruise, and it wasn't hard to consider them friends.

Although Jambor's recollection is from his experience playing in recess, his point about the importance of perceiving teachers as genuine persons applies to the classroom and other educational contexts as well. When teachers present themselves and act as caring human beings as opposed to strict disciplinarians, students learn to trust them, are less likely to engage in disruptive behavior, and more likely to confide in them when a problem arises. Indeed, adults who listen patiently, show an interest in their students' lives, and even apologize for something they regret doing, are modeling for students an ethical way of being with others. What needs to be emphasized here is that being a caring person and forming warm relationships with one's students is inconsistent with trying to control them. Hence, if we accept the premise that educators ought to be genuine persons and develop close relationships with children, it follows that they will have to relinquish the desire to control their students.

But what will happen if teachers stop trying to control their students? Will it result in chaos and anarchy in the classroom? The answer is "not necessarily." Clearly, some sort of structure and order is necessary in a classroom if students are to learn and flourish. Yet, a healthy classroom structure is not contingent on teachers wielding control through some sort of reward and punishment system. Kohn's book *Beyond Discipline* describes in some detail how to establish a caring community in one's classroom, a community that has a structure in place but is not dependent on rules and consequences. Here is not the place to describe all the characteristics of such a community, but only to mention that it is a place where students feel that they are valued and respected and are encouraged to care about each other. The key thing to remember is that the notion of a caring community follows directly from the premise that the relations among educators and students have to be based on care, respect, and open communication. In such a community, behavioral problems are dealt with in collaboration with students in a way that protects the safety and dignity of each individual and does not sacrifice one person's interest for the good of the group.

The increasing use of practices such as do-nows and time on-task as well as the diminished role of recess in many schools should not be viewed as merely a current trend that arises out of the need to enhance learning and prepare students to take the standardized tests. Actually, such practices are grounded on a set of beliefs about the nature of children, knowledge, and the social context — beliefs that are usually taken for granted rather than critically examined. To assume that children cannot be trusted to regulate themselves, that knowledge is a set of facts that has already been discovered, and that the teacher's role is one of creator and enforcer of rules, lead directly to the conclusion that techniques and practices that increase time on-task are needed to manage students' learning and behavior. However, currently there is little credible data that techniques and practices, like do-nows and eliminating recess, have a positive impact on student learning and development.

Moreover, a careful analysis of the underlying assumptions of many of the most popular management theories shows that they do not hold up to close scrutiny. Instead, there is considerable evidence to support the argument that children have the capacity to be generous and compassionate, that knowledge is something that humans construct in collaboration with others, and that mutual respect and care are crucial to promote a healthy learning environment. Embracing the latter set of assumptions implies that we cease to regard the managing and controlling of student behavior as one of the main educational goals. It means that we need to refocus our energies on engaging students in meaningful activities and on collaborating with them to create caring communities that are safe, orderly, and exciting for all students.

NOTE

1. Buber gives the example of a young teacher entering an unruly class for the first time who is tempted to start with disciplining the students and establishing control. However, the teacher manages to make a connection with one of the students and in the process gain the attention and interest of the entire class. See his essay The Education of Character in (Buber 1955).

Chapter Five

Confusion and Uncertainty Hinder Learning

Plato's dialogue, *The Meno*, is a discussion of the nature of virtue and, in particular, the question of whether virtue can be taught. Menon, a wealthy young nobleman, approaches Socrates and asks him the following questions: "Can you tell me, Socrates—can virtue can be taught? Or if not, does it come by practice? Or does it come neither by practice nor by teaching, but do people get it by nature, or in some other way?" (Warmington and Rouse 1956, 28) When Socrates hears these questions, he immediately stops Menon and says to him something like this: "Wait a minute, my dear Menon, how can I talk about whether virtue can or cannot be taught, when I don't even know what virtue *is*!" In other words, Socrates asks: How can I talk about the qualities or attributes of something without first defining it, that is, before having a fairly clear understanding of what this concept means?

Regardless of whether Socrates is actually telling the truth when he claims that he does not know what virtue is, he succeeds in convincing Menon that he does not know and gets the confident young nobleman to attempt to define virtue. And so in the opening pages of the dialogue, Menon makes several attempts to define virtue, all of which are ultimately refuted by Socrates. In some cases, Socrates rejects Menon's explanations because they are actually particular examples or parts of virtue and not a general definition of the concept as a whole. In other cases, Socrates shows that what Menon has offered is illogical or does not make sense. Finally, after failing at numerous attempts to define virtue,

Menon becomes very frustrated with Socrates and admits that he is confused and even stunned.

> And now you seem to me to be a regular wizard, you dose me
> with drugs and bewitch me with charms and spells, and
> drown me in puzzledom.... Really and truly, my soul is numb
> and my mouth is numb, and what to answer you I do not
> know. Yet I have a thousand times made long speeches about
> virtue, before many a large audience, and good speeches, too,
> as I was convinced; but now I have not a word to say at all as
> to what it is. (Warmington and Rouse 1956, 40)

Clearly, Menon is in an uncomfortable state of mind now, a state of bewilderment and frustration that people usually find very disturbing. Yet one way to interpret the process that Menon goes through is to consider the possibility that, educationally speaking, he may be better off in his present state of confusion and numbness than when he thought he knew what virtue meant. At the beginning of the dialogue, Menon came across as very confident and sure of himself; he was not really open to examine his beliefs about virtue, merely repeating his already formed ideas. After Socrates demonstrates that all of his ideas about virtue are problematic, Menon begins to doubt himself and to question many of the beliefs he previously took for granted. Confused and facing his own limitations, Menon is now much more open and willing than he was before to search together with Socrates for a good definition of virtue.

What implication for teaching and learning can be gleaned from this particular interpretation of what happens to Menon? One noteworthy lesson is that, while the state of confusion may be psychologically uncomfortable or unsettling, educationally speaking it is not necessarily a bad thing. Indeed, being confused and perplexed can often lead us to search deeper, to question previously cherished beliefs, and to take on a new perspective. In contrast, when we are sure that we understand and know something, we are much less likely to examine it critically. Yet such examinations are essential, as the dialogues of Plato illustrate, because they usually lead to a deeper and more complex understanding of the concept or issue that is being investigated. In short, what I am suggesting is that teachers who embrace confusion, uneasiness, and a sense of wonder in their classrooms are helping, rather than hurting, their students. In this chapter, I would like to use this insight to challenge an established educational belief that uncertainty hurts students and that students' learning is stifled when they are confused.

CLEAR EXPECTATIONS ENHANCE LEARNING

Consider the following passage from a popular classroom management book about the significance of providing clear instruction to students:

> Communicating information and directions in a clear, comprehensible manner is an important teaching skill. Clear instruction helps students learn faster and more successfully; it also helps students understand your directions and expectations for behavior more readily. Although clarity is important in all classroom activities, it is crucial during content development when nearly all new subject matter is introduced and taught. (Evertson, Emmer, and Worsham 2000, 103)

Both new and veteran teachers who read this passage will probably consider the ideas presented in it as self-evident, reasonable, or just plain common sense. Almost all teachers experience in some way or other the problem that is alluded to in this passage: that students are confused about what is expected of them because the teachers' instructions were vague or indecisive. Thus, clear instruction enables students to understand how teachers expect them to behave and, even more importantly, the specific content that they are supposed to learn.

What are some of the essential factors required for instruction to be clear? Evertson, Emmer, and Worsham maintain that clear instruction involves the coherent organization of information; the use of a sufficient amount of examples; presentations that are concrete and precise; constant monitoring of student comprehension; and providing students enough practice to ensure mastery. They elaborate this point writing that

> clarity involves stating goals or major objectives and making sure that students know what they are accountable for knowing or doing; carefully outlining a lesson sequence, moving from simpler to more complex ideas; providing instructions both orally and in writing; checking understanding by asking specific questions or obtaining work samples; and providing for meaningful practice and feedback through classwork or

homework assignments that review all lesson skills and content. (Evertson, Emmer, and Worsham 2000, 103)

Summarizing more than a decade of research about teacher impact on student achievement, Brophy (1986, 1071) concludes that "students learn more when their teachers' presentations are *clear* rather than vague or rambling and when they are delivered with *enthusiasm*." This research suggests that students learn more when the information is coherently structured and when there is a sufficient amount of repetition of the main ideas or concepts. Brophy's study indicates that learning suffers when teachers fail to pursue any clear objectives, ask vague or ambiguous questions, and do not provide enough direct supervision for their students.

Given the widespread conception that clear instruction enhances learning and comprehension of the subject matter, it is not surprising that many students are turned off by teachers who do not communicate in a coherent manner. Who has not experienced a class taught by a confused and unorganized teacher? My own memory of such a class is clear, though the subject matter that was taught is nebulous at best. This particular class, titled "Politics and Education," was an elective course I took in graduate school as part of a doctorate program in Philosophy and Education. The professor, who seemed frequently unprepared, had a very passive and unenthusiastic approach to teaching. He would walk into the classroom, pose a question to the entire class about one of the texts, and then facilitate a discussion about this question that turned into tedious free association after about fifteen minutes. Although discussions can be very exciting and fruitful, in this class they were always unfocused and did not seem to lead to any new insights. The professor never took charge of the discussion during the two-hour class and seemed himself confused about the goals of the course. Other students in the class shared my frustration with the professor and with the wandering and aimless nature of the conversations we had. The only thing I remember about the content of this course is writing a term paper about Machiavelli.

THE PURPOSE OF EDUCATION AND THE NATURE OF REALITY

In light of the discussion above, it would seem extremely difficult to challenge the claim that clear expectations and instruction enhance

learning and that confusion hurts students. However, problems, as is often the case, begin to arise when we dig a little deeper and look closely at
the details that lie beneath the general ideas. One problem that comes to
mind is that achievement and performance on standardized tests are often mistaken for genuine learning and understanding. Making the case
for clear and organized instruction, Brophy insists that achievement is
maximized when teachers structure the material coherently, highlight
the main ideas, and review these ideas at the end of the lesson (Brophy
1986, 1071). Yet the nature and quality of this achievement is never really
spelled out in any detail. Is achievement supposed to be understood as
the ability to display various facts and skills at a particular moment in
time? Is it the capacity to apply these facts and skills to some unfamiliar
situation? Or, finally, does achievement actually imply that a person has
mastered these facts and skills and is prepared to use them in any situation?

Ted Sizer (1996, 44-45) argues correctly that, historically speaking, academic achievement has been equated primarily with the first of these
categories and sometimes with the second. The third, he maintains, is
largely ignored, though many people would agree that the acquisition of
intellectual habits of mind is the hallmark of real learning and that
schools are supposed to cultivate these habits. People who share this
view typically hold that being an educated citizen means that one is able
to think critically, consider issues from multiple perspectives, and make
sound judgments based on reliable evidence. For Sizer, schools should
help students become "respectful skeptics, accustomed to asking 'Why?'
and being satisfied only with an answer that has as solid a base of evidence as possible" (Sizer 1996, 76). Now, if we accept Sizer's view that
schools ought to foster people who are respectful skeptics, it follows that
students will have to practice asking tough questions and carefully justifying their beliefs. Like Socrates and his dialogue partners, students
need to engage in a continuous process of inquiry in which their basic beliefs and those of others are subjected to close scrutiny.

What I am suggesting here is that in order to gain genuine knowledge
about anything, it is essential to undergo an active process of inquiry,
which involves questioning, doubting, and reexamining one's beliefs. In
the course of this process, it is almost inevitable that one will become perplexed, as Menon did, yet the confusion is an impetus for further investigation. Indeed, the history of science, philosophy, and ideas in general
indicates that human advancement has come when people were con-

fused about something and insisted on asking "Why?" and "How?" As Sizer (1996, 78) notes, "progress comes from seeing something new and compelling in the apparently familiar, teasing out fresh and often better conclusions on the basis of fresh and diligently sought-after evidence."

What is evident from those researchers who call on teachers to ensure that their expectations and delivery are crystal clear is that the teacher is supposed to be very active: to structure, organize, explain, highlight, summarize, and review the content. Yet no such requirements are placed on the students, who are regarded as largely passive and expected to follow the lead of the teacher and memorize the information that she transmits. The problem is that once students grow accustomed to merely following the prescriptions of others, it is extremely difficult to get them to be more active and to take responsibility for their own learning. Loughran and Northfield (1996, 37), for instance, have shown that once students learn to expect to be taught in a teacher-directed way, they resist when they are confronted by teachers who challenge them to think for themselves. Since it is much easier to rely on the teacher to be the source of knowledge, moving out of their comfort zone and trying to work out solutions to problems for themselves is something that many students do not enjoy doing.

In the course of their schooling, most students learn not only that it is easier to let the teacher generate the knowledge in the classroom but also that success is attained by giving the "right answers" to the assigned tasks. Northfield and Loughran (1996, 128) expand on this point noting that

> in one sense, the greater the certainty associated with the task, the easier (and safer) it is for students to pursue success as they know what they are aiming for. It is interesting to note that when learning tasks move away from being clear and rigid, students begin to become suspicious of change. This can happen when the tasks involve enjoyment. Paradoxically, the introduction of interest and enjoyment in learning can be a signal to students that the demands are changing and that they should be "on their guard."

My own experience confirms Loughran and Northfield's point about students becoming suspicious of change when the requirements are flexible and make room for choice and creativity. Many students became anxious when they were expected to take responsibility for their own learning and suggested that they would prefer if I told them exactly what they needed to learn.]

To be sure, clear expectations and unambiguous assignments make things easier not only for the students but also for teachers who can thereby limit the unexpected occurrences in the classroom, save time, and cover more content. However, saving time and making life easier for teachers are probably not the most important educational objectives. As in many debates, everything hinges on what one considers the underlying purpose of education. If the main purpose of education is to prepare students to take standardized tests in the most efficient way possible, then clear expectations and instruction are certainly needed to achieve this goal. But if, as I advocate, the primary aim is to cultivate critical and creative thinkers and caring individuals, then the emphasis will need to shift to those methods and techniques that facilitate active learning, inquiry, and self-examination.

Besides, we need to keep in mind that human reality and our everyday experience are marked by surprises and that they cannot be characterized in black-and-white or clear-cut terms. Indeed, this reality is full of controversies, ambiguities, shades of gray, and uncertainties. There is never just one way to analyze an event in history, a Shakespearean play, a problem in science, or for that matter, an argument between two friends. In fact, what makes human existence so fascinating and meaningful are precisely the ambiguities, struggles, complexities, and contradictions that characterize our lives.

Given the uncertain, complex nature of human reality, it stands to reason that we need to seriously question the claim that instruction should always be clear and that confusion hurts students. Are teachers not undermining their students' ability to gain a deep understanding of this reality when they present the subject matter in a clear-cut and one-dimensional way? When Christopher Columbus, for example, is presented as simply the courageous European who discovered the new world, as many history textbooks do, are we not robbing children of the opportunity to come to a critical historical awareness of the conquest of the Americas? And when a Robert Frost poem is considered from a single perspective (i.e., the teacher's), will many teenagers, who face confusion and doubt every day, not come away thinking that poetry is not for them because it has nothing to do with their lived experience?

I raise these questions not for the sake of providing a conclusive answer, but to call attention to the tension between the claim that teachers'

expectations and instruction should be crystal clear and the nature of human reality, which is uncertain and multifaceted. The lesson to learn here
is *not* that teachers should deliberately try to confuse students so that
they will better adjust to the ambiguous and complex nature of our existence. It is rather that, as teachers, we should not shy away from moments of perplexity and uncertainty in our lessons because such
moments are opportunities to investigate further and consider problems
from fresh perspectives. In doing so, we will be modeling for our students that a sense of confusion and doubt needs to be embraced, not
avoided, as it is likely to result in a deeper awareness of ourselves and
our relationship to the world around us.

Moreover, since there is always a gap between what teachers teach
and what students actually learn, some level of confusion is inherent in
every classroom interaction. That is, the information, directions, and
messages that teachers communicate are never understood by all students in the exact way that teachers intend them to be heard. Even if a
teacher conveys the ideas in the clearest possible way, there is always a
certain measure of confusion and uncertainty in the classroom. This is
due to the fact that every student is a unique individual and therefore
each one interprets and makes sense of the information in a slightly different way. The fact that a measure of uncertainty is inherent in every
student-teacher interaction reinforces the point that we should embrace
rather than shy away from moments of confusion. By embracing confusion, both teachers and students will gradually learn to take advantage
of moments of perplexity in order to dig deeper, consider alternative
ideas, and attempt new methods that have not yet been explored.

TEACHING TO EMBRACE UNCERTAINTY

In one of the opening scenes of the film *Dead Poets Society*, Robin Williams, a new teacher in the school, takes his students out of the classroom
on the first day into one of the halls of the boarding school where photos
of previous graduating classes are hanging on the wall. Williams asks
one of the students to read the first stanza of a poem whose message is
seize the day, or *carpe diem* in Latin. He then prompts the students to reflect on why the poet is urging the reader to seize the day. Receiving no
response, Williams states emphatically that it is "because we are all food
for worms, lads, because, believe it or not, each one of us in this room will
one day stop breathing, turn cold, and die." The scene ends with Williams getting the students to look closely at the pictures on the wall while

he stands behind them and creepily whispers in their ears to "seize the day boys, make your life extraordinary."

Set in a preparatory boarding school in the 1950s, William's teaching approach stands in stark contrast to the traditional model practiced by all the other teachers and endorsed by the school administration. While all the other professors focus on drilling the students in their subjects and preparing them for the college entrance exams, Williams attempts to educate them to think for themselves, find their own voices, and strive to realize their true desires. Initially, many of the boys are puzzled and even taken aback by William's approach. Yet, gradually more and more students come to understand and appreciate Williams's goals.

What can we learn about the notion that teaching should embrace uncertainty from this short scene from the movie *Dead Poets Society*? Williams was undoubtedly the kind of teacher who was not preoccupied with clarity and certainty; he was quite comfortable with ambiguities, confusion, and doubt. Indeed, he wanted to provoke his students to question, to take risks, and to think for themselves. Williams pursues this goal by taking his students out of their familiar classroom setting, their comfort zone, and thrusting them into an unknown situation in which they are immediately asked to reflect on a pretty tough question, look closely at some pictures, and listen to his spooky message. Even before he took the students out to the hall, he came into the classroom unexpectedly from a back door whistling a tune. On other occasions, Williams does some pretty shocking things like jumping abruptly on top of his desk to illustrate the importance of always taking a new perspective.

What I am suggesting is that Williams's actions in the scene described above, as well as many of his other scenes throughout this film, provide some good examples of teaching students to embrace uncertainty. In effect, he continuously models for his students how to welcome the unfamiliar, by himself taking risks, going against the norms of the school, and by integrating passion and excitement into the study of English. Williams clearly takes a risk when he instructs the students on one of the first days of school to rip out of their textbooks the entire introduction because the author is describing how to measure poetry. And he integrates excitement into the study of Shakespeare, regarded as boring by many high school students, by using passion and impersonation when reading his sonnets and plays. The point here is not that teachers should try to imitate Williams to teach students to embrace uncertainty and confusion. Rather it is that, like Williams, we need to constantly attempt to

challenge the boundaries of what is considered normal teaching practice.

In confronting and crossing these boundaries, teachers will frequently enter into uncharted and uncertain ground. However, the journey will take them and their students into places that reach far beyond
the traditional model, a model that prizes clarity and determination and
assesses learning through test results. In Williams's case, challenging the
limits of conventional teaching practice enabled some of his students to
become more aware of themselves, think independently, and attain their
true calling. That is, teaching to embrace uncertainty can create possibilities for students that were previously not available for them. As bell
hooks (1994, 207) puts it:

> The classroom, with all its limitations, remains a location of
> possibility. In that field of possibility we have the opportu-
> nity to labor for freedom, to demand of ourselves and our
> comrades, an openness of mind and heart that allows us to
> face reality even as we collectively imagine ways to move be-
> yond boundaries, to transgress.

Another way of helping students learn to embrace uncertainty is by
giving the arts a central role in the curriculum of schools. The arts,
whether we are talking about literature, painting, music or film, are
unique in that they call our attention to the complexities, ambiguities,
and uncertainties of human existence. The confusion and indecisiveness
of Hamlet, the complexity of a John Coltrane tune, the mysteriousness of
a Corbet landscape, and the struggles of the heroine in the film *Frida* —
all capture something fundamental about what it means to be human.
They do this by making manifest a range of perspectives on the human
condition, many of which may not have been visible to us before. Maxine
Greene, who for decades has been one of the most vocal advocates for integrating the arts into the curriculum, argues that giving the arts a central role will "nurture a ground for enhanced wide-awakeness and
thoughtfulness and consciousness of one another" (Greene 2000, 13). In
Greene's view, the arts are essential because they help us become more
aware of the deficiencies of our existence and because they open our
imagination to new possibilities for transforming our lives for the better.

Educating students to welcome confusion can also be done through a
kind of investigation and questioning that promotes uncertainty.
Thinking back on those teachers who had the most impact on me, I real-

ized that most, if not all, of them were skilled at asking very profound, open-ended questions. The questions they asked usually did not have easy and clear-cut answers. Rather, they were complex and difficult problems that lent themselves to multiple interpretations and stimulated diverse opinions and intense discussion. Much like the dialogues of Plato, these discussions typically did not produce any conclusive answers to the questions that were raised. But the process of debating these complex and confusing problems always led me and my classmates to a deeper understanding of the underlying issues. Ultimately, debating these tough questions taught me the value of being skeptical, of doubting the familiar, of not being content with simple answers, and of searching for alternative viewpoints.

In light of the insights of Williams, hooks, and Greene, as well as my own experience, teachers need to remember that precisely because human existence is not certain or predetermined, children should have the opportunity to go beyond ordinary and accepted norms. This implies that as teachers we need to strive to create opportunities for our students that enable them to confront confusions and uncertainties and to explore new alternatives. Greene calls these opportunities "spaces" and rightly insists that if spaces can be opened that disclose alternative realities or ways of being,

> individuals are far more likely to break with the ordinary and the taken-for-granted. Visions may appear before their mind's eye — visions of what might be, what ought to be. Experiences of this kind are what direct attention to deficiencies, the inequalities in lived situations; they may, in fact, provoke persons to take action together — to transcend the deficiencies, to transform. (Greene 2000, 8-9)

CONCLUSION

In putting so much emphasis on clear expectations and instruction, there is a serious danger that we may be teaching our children to avoid tough questions, confusion, and a sense of wonder about the world. Being content with a narrow definition of achievement, schools are, in effect, training students not to think too deeply about important issues, problems, and events. Perhaps schools would be better off embracing confusion and uncertainty. Perhaps those teachers who are doing this and who knowingly ask their students complex and perplexing questions are doing them a service. Indeed, I would argue that they are educating their students to doubt, think critically, to consider issues from multiple perspectives, and to provide convincing arguments for their views.

These goals are far from trivial; as a matter of fact, without them our democracy is in jeopardy. One could probably make a pretty strong case that one of the main reasons that our democracy is currently being eroded in the United States and that so few people are involved in politics is that our nation's schools, media, and other institutions that educate people are not doing their jobs. Rather than teaching people to be critical thinkers and respectful skeptics, these institutions are educating them to accept information that is given them without question, to look for simplistic solutions to complex problems, and to adjust to the status quo. The majority of the mainstream media in the United States, for instance, presents the news in a very superficial, one-sided, and mundane way. An atrocity in Africa or Asia gets less attention than the transgressions of celebrities in this country. Without a critical awareness and a complex understanding of social and political issues, individuals will not be able to exercise their right to be active citizens and participators in our democracy. Such an awareness and understanding can only come about if we educate our citizens to embrace confusion and uncertainty and consider a wide range of perspectives before making judgments.

Chapter Six

Technology Is the Cure for All Problems in Education

Since the early 1980s billions of dollars in federal funding have been poured into computerizing schools in the United States and making them more technologically advanced. According to Larry Cuban, who has researched this topic extensively, "in 1981 there were, on average, 125 students per computer in U.S. schools. A decade later, the ratio was 18 to 1. By 2000 it had dropped to 5 students per computer" (Cuban 2001, 17). Yet, funding for new computer hardware and software for schools is only part of the huge investment made in the technological revolution we are witnessing. Other costs include paying for technical support, professional development of teachers and staff, and the scheduled replacement of obsolete equipment. All in all, we are talking about a multibillion dollar investment each year that is currently competing with other educational needs, such as smaller class size, higher entry-level teacher salaries, and the renovation of decayed buildings.

This huge investment in technology reflects the goals of business leaders, academics, and educational policymakers at the highest levels of government. For instance, Cuban (2001, 16) points out that in 1996 President Clinton challenged the nation to achieve four objectives:

- Modern computers and learning devices will be accessible to every student.
- Classrooms will be connected to one another and to the outside world.

- Educational software will be an integral part of the curriculum —
  and as engaging as the best videogame.
- Teachers will be ready to use and teach with technology.

These objectives, as well as the major investment in computerizing schools that ensued from them, rest on a set of unexamined assumptions that need to be carefully scrutinized. First, it was assumed that the increased availability of technology in schools and classrooms would lead to its increased use. Second, it was asserted that increased use would result in better teaching and learning as well as higher student achievement on standardized tests. Finally, this implies that students would become more educated and better citizens as a result of the integration of technology into teaching and learning. This chapter critically analyzes each of these assumptions and argues that they are not supported by the existing evidence. My analysis suggests that educators need to reexamine their position on computers in the classroom so that they will become more aware of the real implications of the technological revolution and the advantages and the limitations of these tools.

ABUNDANT ACCESS, LITTLE USE

The invention of powerful computers and information technologies are by no means the first technological advances that were supposed to bring about a major reform in schooling. Indeed, as Cuban shows, previous advances in the twentieth century — the development of film, radio, and instructional television — were also greeted with high expectations for transforming teaching and learning. Much like computers, these earlier technologies were touted as effective solutions for many of the problems that schools faced. "For example, in the 1950s promoters of instructional television hailed that new technology as a solution to a teacher shortage at that time" (Cuban 2001, 137). Yet Cuban's analysis found that in most cases the use of film, radio, and instructional television tended to be infrequent among teachers, limited to perpetuating existing practices, and peripheral to the daily routines of teaching and learning.

The limited use of earlier technologies by teachers can be accounted for in large part by the fact that most schools and teachers had inadequate access to these technologies. Cuban cites issues such as scheduling difficulties and the incompatibility between the existing curriculum and the offerings of films, radio, and television to support teachers' complaints about the technology being inaccessible. But this explanation cannot be so easily applied to the infrequent use of computers in most public schools today across the nation. Although teachers in many districts have far greater access to information technologies and better training than their predecessors did, the existing research still suggests that there is rather limited use of computer and information technologies in most classrooms. Moreover, this limited use is even more surprising given the fact that many of the same teachers who have not integrated technology into their classrooms are much more likely to make use of some of the same technology at home.

Why is that the case? Why has the enthusiasm of the educational policymakers, administrators, and business leaders not resulted in more widespread use of the new technologies? Cuban offers a number of explanations, each of which may partially account for this phenomenon, but the one that I find particularly convincing is what he called the "historical, social, organizational, and political context of teaching." This explanation is persuasive since it attributes the gap between home and school use of technology to "the social and political organization of schooling, societal expectations for schools, and historical legacies, all of which influence what occurs in classrooms" (Cuban 2001, 156). This account makes sense because it considers teaching not as an isolated activity that individuals perform in classrooms, but as part of the larger social, historical, political, and economic context that shapes the work of teachers and schools. Such a perspective is essential, as John Dewey (1956, 7) suggests in *The School and Society*, because it gives us a broader and more accurate picture of the issues and struggles that teachers face.

To understand the impact of this larger context on teachers' reluctance to use the available technology, consider the following issues that are common in secondary schools:

> separate classrooms, individual departments, age-graded groupings, and six-period work day. Add the time spent by each teacher to work out the logistics necessary to bring classes to media centers and computer labs. Then factor in nervousness over possible server crashes, software foul-ups, printer glitches, and slow Internet connections. Any high school teacher who manages to use computers in the classroom has somehow overcome a host of organizational problems, political decisions made by others remote from the

classroom, and difficulties associated with the technology itself.... (Cuban 2001, 173)

The difficulties referred to above include the deployment of new increasingly complex software that is not designed to take into account
teachers' practical needs. Generally speaking, there seems to be a big
mismatch between the demand to integrate technology into teachers'
lessons and the fact that most schools are not very flexible and accommo-
dating places in which to work.

In addition, virtually all of the studies I surveyed regarded the challenges and time constraints placed on teachers as serious enough to prevent many of them from using technology in their classrooms. For
instance, Russell and his colleagues (2003, 308) interviewed over 100
principals suggested that because new teachers have to "develop behavior management techniques, become familiar with the curriculum,
adapt to the school culture, and become familiar with the assessment
systems — they do not have time to explore ways to integrate the technology available to them." These findings clearly indicate that if we
want teachers to integrate technology into their lessons, it is not enough
to put computers in schools and make them available to teachers. To
have them used, we first need to alleviate some of the pressures and time
constraints placed on teachers.

Besides time constraints, numerous studies point to another important problem that impedes the use of technology for instructional purposes among new teachers: "Although newer teachers are generally
familiar and comfortable with working with technology, they have not
been exposed to applications of technology in the classroom" (Russell et
al. 2003, 308). While many of these teachers grew up working with technology at home and in other settings, they themselves as K–12 students
had little experience with models of teaching based on the integration of
technology into the classroom. Even in their teacher education programs, most teacher candidates were taught how to use the available
technology (e.g., PowerPoint and the Internet) rather than how to teach
with technology and integrate it into their lessons. This means that while
new teachers tend to be comfortable with technology and commonly use
it in their everyday lives, they don't know how to use this technology to
enhance learning.

All these reasons — the broader social context of teaching, time constraints, pressures teacher face, and the lack of training in the application

of technology to the classroom — contribute to the fact that, although computer technologies are abundant and accessible in many schools, most teachers use them in a very limited way, if they use them at all. As Janet Schofield and Ann Davidson (2002, 13) point out in their book, *Bringing the Internet to School*, "Internet access does not guarantee Internet use, and it seems obvious that use must occur for there to be any realistic possibility of sustained positive outcomes." Schofield and Davidson's study, as well as those of the other researchers cited above, all call into question one of the central myths about the utilization of technology in schools: that increased availability of computers in schools and classrooms would automatically result in the increased use of this technology.

INCREASE USE OF TECHNOLOGY MEANS BETTER STUDENT OUTCOMES

A second assumption regarding the integration of computer technology into schools and classrooms is that increased use of this technology will result in better teaching and learning, as well as higher student achievement on standardized tests. For instance, in a recent report that summarizes the impact of technology on student achievement, Apple Computer (2002/2003, 42) claimed that

> studies have shown that students with routine access to *technology* learn these basic skills faster and better when they have a chance to practice them using *technology*. One of the reasons cited for this improvement is that students are engaged by the *technology*. As a result, they spend more time learning and practicing the basic tasks than students who approach the same tasks in a traditional paper-and-pencil manner. Students are more motivated to learn when *technology* is part of their daily school experience.

This bold statement was made by the Apple Computer — which in itself raises some serious questions about the impartiality of the research conclusions. In an insightful article, "Toward a Theory of Negativity: Teacher Education and Information and Communications Technology," Heather-Jane Robertson (2003, 281) cites this statement and points out that its authors rest their assertions on a 1997 report that also was produced by Apple. The fact that Apple has a vested interest in promoting the proliferation of computer technologies in schools together with the finding that the 2002 report is based on Apple's own prior research, should leave us wondering about the accuracy of the results. Sweeping generalizations such as "students are more motivated to learn when technology is part of their daily school experience" suggest that the conclusion has been established beyond any reasonable doubt and is not open to debate. However, I submit that the assumption that increased use of computer technologies in schools will result in better teaching and learning as well as in higher student achievement needs to be carefully examined.

Let us first look closely at the narrower claim, namely, that increased use of technology will lead to higher achievement scores on standardized tests. Virtually all of the studies that I have looked at did not find a significant correlation between a wider access to technology and higher achievement levels. Cuban (2001, 178), for instance, argues that "there have been no advances (measured by higher academic achievement of urban, suburban, or rural students) over the last decade that can be confidently attributed to broader access to computers." Likewise, Schofield and Davidson (2002, 311) assert that "there is little reason to believe that Internet use can be expected to have a strong effect on students' performance on the kinds of standardized tests typically used to measure achievement in school subjects." Studies conducted in other countries besides the United States have also come to the same conclusion. For example, a report (Fielding 2003) of a four-year, comprehensive, government-funded study in England uncovered "no consistent relationship between computer use and pupil achievement in any subject at any age."

Why is it that the effect of computer technology is so minimal in the classroom? Several possible reasons come to mind. First, is the unexpected outcome discovered by Cuban and his associates in their research with various schools in Silicon Valley that the overwhelming majority of teachers surveyed used the available technology to maintain existing patterns of teaching rather than making fundamental changes. In Cuban's (2001, 96-97) words:

> If anything, what we observed and were told by students suggested strongly that occasional to serious use of computers in their classes had marginal or no impact on routine teaching practices. In other words, most teachers had adapted an innovation to fit their customary practices, not to revolutionize

them. Most teachers who adopted technologies such as overhead projectors, VCR's, instructional television, laser disk
players, and computers tailor the use of these machines to fit
the familiar practices of teacher-centered instruction.

Cuban's findings suggest, therefore, that since the vast majority of teachers who integrated technology into their lessons did so to fit existing practices rather than innovate, it is plausible to conclude that such use of
technology would have little or no effect on student achievement. In other
words, since teaching practices have not changed dramatically with the
introduction of computers in schools, there is little reason to expect students to perform much differently on standardized tests.

Another important reason for the finding that increased use of technology does not result in higher academic achievement is that such improvement is not often the primary objective of teachers who integrate
technology. Commenting on Internet use, Schofield and Davidson
(2002, 311-312) point out that other goals such as preparing students to
live in a technological world, expanding students' global awareness,
and supporting interdisciplinary curriculum initiatives tend to be a
higher priority for teachers than increased achievement. In short, "although increased academic achievement might be a by-product of
Internet use in the service of other goals, such an outcome does not
seem likely unless teachers specifically seek it, and even then the link-
age is not inevitable." I suspect that this statement is equally true of
other computer technologies such as teachers' use of PowerPoint and
discussion boards in their teaching.

What about the broader claim that the more teachers use computer
technologies in schools, the better the teaching and learning will be?
Again, my analysis indicates that the evidence for this claim is ambiguous rather than clear-cut and open to interpretation rather than self-evident. For instance, Schofield and Davidson (2002, 253) report that "for
students, the clearest and most consistent outcome connected to Internet
use was an increase in their enjoyment of their time in school and in their
motivation." Yet students' use of the Internet is not the only activity that
can increase their enjoyment of school and their motivation to learn.
Clearly, there are other hands-on and inquiry-based activities, such as
science labs and art classes that produce similar results. Hence, increasing students' motivation and enjoyment depends much more on transforming the culture of schools from one in which students are mere

passive consumers of information to one that challenges them to be active doers and researchers. However, this insight is hardly new and can be traced back at the very least to John Dewey and the Progressive Education movement of the late nineteenth and early twentieth centuries. It is simply incorrect to suggest, as the Apple report does, that using technology is the only activity that engages students and increases their motivation in schools.

Moreover, Schofield and Davidson (2002, 234) conclude that giving students access to the Internet has its drawbacks in that it can serve as a temptation that shifts attention from the topic of the day to various unrelated issues:

> In traditional classroom situations, students may daydream, fall asleep, or chat with peers, but they do not have virtually instant access to a huge archive of competing material that many find enthralling. Thus, the same resource that appears to increase work-related motivation also presents an unparalleled temptation and opportunity to turn to material unrelated to work.

Although different from the drudgery of traditional education, integrating the Internet into one's teaching can provide students with a distraction that easily takes them away from the purpose and focus of the lesson.

To further illustrate the problem with the claim that increased use of computer technologies in schools will necessarily result in better teaching and learning, consider the use of PowerPoint presentations in instruction. Granted that teaching a lesson with PowerPoint enables the teacher to create a visually stimulating image that can capture students' attention and keep them focused on the lesson, there are nevertheless some critical problems with this technology. To begin with, PowerPoint presentations are typically used to perpetuate teacher-centered instruction in which the goal is to transmit a good chunk of information to the students in an efficient time frame. Since, like more traditional chalk-and-talk lessons, these presentations attempt to present a lot of ideas in a relatively short amount of time, the result is that many of the ideas being conveyed are not absorbed by the students. I have witnessed numerous PowerPoint presentations flounder, precisely because the teachers tried to get across too much information in a short lesson. Instead of focusing on presenting a few ideas in depth and generating a discussion about them, these presentations at best succeed in merely "covering" the material.

My discussions with other teachers and my own observations also indicate that this technology can be more constraining and inflexible than more traditional teaching tools. For instance, a high school math teacher commented that he prefers using the blackboard and chalk in his lessons to both an overhead projector and PowerPoint since the former gives him much more flexibility. He explained that by using the blackboard he is able to illustrate the dynamic development of a problem to his students, whereas the other two technologies often skip the development or give you merely a glimpse of it. The point is that with an overhead projector and PowerPoint the students are usually able to view only one slide at any given moment and that each slide is replaced by the next one rather quickly. In contrast, when using the blackboard the students can view the entire process of solving a problem from beginning to end, thereby enabling them to refer back more easily to a step they missed or are confused about. Contrary to the claims of the technophiles, there appear to be at least some instances in which using computers in instruction give both teachers and students less flexibility and spontaneity compared to more traditional methods of teaching.

In sum, the evidence suggests that increased use of computer technologies in instruction is neither a solution for raising test scores nor a remedy for the poor teaching and learning that takes place in many of our nation's schools. Much like other technological advances that preceded them, computers are merely tools that when used thoughtfully can enhance teaching and learning. For instance, the Internet can "create new opportunities for learning by bringing real-world problems into the classroom, by letting students find problems to study as well as solving problems that educators set for them, and by letting students interact with experts in a variety of ways" (Schofield and Davidson 2002, 312). On the other hand, computer technologies can also be employed (and are often used) in ways that perpetuate traditional, teacher-centered instruction, thereby not challenging students and keeping them passive. Moreover, as with earlier inventions used in education, the new technologies bring with them a significant downside that needs to be acknowledged rather than ignored. Instead of embracing the new technologies blindly, a careful and honest analysis of integrating computers into schools and classrooms will therefore need to examine both their benefits and limitations.

MORE TECHNOLOGY MEANS BETTER EDUCATION

The final assumption that I wish to examine here is that students will become more educated and better citizens as a result of the integration of technology into schools and classrooms. This last assertion is particularly troubling not only because it is taken for granted by many teachers, administrators, and policymakers but also because it is based on belief or ideology rather than hard evidence. As such, it is the kind of statement that is very difficult to refute scientifically. To illustrate such a belief, consider the following statement made by David Dwyer (1996, 31) about the role of technology with respect to "at-risk" children:

> Half of America's children engage in behaviors that place them in serious risk of alienation, even of death. [These children believe] that they are not wanted and are of little value in this society. Technology is the only vehicle we may ride as we work to engage more children in the excitement and life-enhancing experiences of learning.

First of all, the problem with this statement is the assertion that using technology is the *only* means of getting students excited about learning, as though there are no other ways to achieve this goal. Such an assertion is reductionistic in that it claims that a very complex problem (the alienation of children) has only one solution (technology). Historically speaking, this assertion makes no sense since we know that the problem of alienation among children is not new and that attempts have already been made to address this issue with varying degrees of success before computer technology was around. Yet perhaps what is most troubling about the claim that technology is the only way to deal with student alienation is that it assumes that the sources of this problem have already been identified and understood. Such a presumption implies that there is no reason to ask *why* and *how* the alienation of children arises and that we can immediately proceed to implement the remedy, namely, technology. However, as with any serious issue, we cannot even begin to address this problem until we acquire a good understanding of its underlying causes.

My intention here is not to explore the historical and social reasons for the alienation of children, but it is important to at least mention that some people believe that technology, far from being the solution, is part of the cause of the problem. Neil Postman, for instance, argues that although the invention of computer technologies in the twentieth century has eliminated the problem of information scarcity, these machines have exacerbated the problem of alienation by creating "information glut," a phenomenon never experienced before. For Postman, information glut contributes to our alienation from the world and human values by transforming "information into a form of garbage, and ourselves into garbage collectors." He explains that, as a result of this glut,

> the tie between information and human purpose has been severed. Information is now a commodity that is bought and sold; it comes indiscriminately, whether asked or not, directed at no one in particular, in enormous volume, at high speeds, disconnected from meaning and import. It comes unquestioned and uncombined, and we do not have ... a loom to weave it all into fabric. No transcendent narratives to provide us with moral guidance, social purpose, intellectual economy. No stories to tell us what we need to know, and especially what we do *not* need to know. (Postman 1997, 29)

The myth that technology provides the best remedy for much of what is wrong with education today has had a significant impact on the daily work of teachers. Robertson writes about a kindergarten teacher who was admonished by her principal because the children were not using all the computers in her classroom when he walked by. Another teacher received a reprimand from her principal because she had "suggested that instead of buying more computers with the funds volunteers had raised, parents might consider buying books and musical instruments" (Robertson 2003, 283).

Bryson and de Castell (1998, 544) point out that

> teachers who are perceived as hesitant, or who experience difficulties with the implementation of "educational change" in this kind of top-down project, accordingly, will be understood as "resisting" educational innovation; they may be characterized, for instance, as "reluctant users," or as "Luddites," in need of some kind of intervention facilitative of an "attitude change" with respect to new technologies.

From this perspective, refusal to implement new technologies in education is a negative action indicating an unwillingness to learn and grow rather than a thoughtful choice or a healthy skepticism.

Yet maintaining a healthy skepticism regarding the role that computer technology can play in education is crucial since, as Robertson suggests, there seems to be a lack of informed, engaged, and critical discussion on the issue. Indeed, in *The Child and the Machine: Why Computers may Put Our Children's Education at Risk*, Armstrong and Casement (2000, 2) observe that

> some of the most elementary questions about the educational use of computers remain unanswered. Why should children be exposed to computer technology from an early age? Are computers and computer software so essential to children's education? What can we expect them to gain? What do they stand to lose? Not only are these issues unresolved, but for the most part the questions themselves have never been asked.

The lack of informed and critical debate on these issues is particularly troubling in light of the fact that technology is viewed by many as the only legitimate remedy that can save public education from disaster. Yet, as Cuban (2001, 189) points out, "the most serious problems afflicting urban and rural poor schools — inequitable funding, extraordinary health and social needs growing out of poverty, crumbling facilities, unqualified teachers — have little to do with a lack of technology." Still, more technology use in schools is often proposed as the cure to such problems because it is easier to talk about a technical solution to this social plague than to face up to the fact that racism and discrimination are alive and well in the United States and are responsible for the difference in opportunities in education. Jonathan Kozol has vividly described such injustices in his 1992 book *Savage Inequalities*, a study that documents the horrific conditions in some of the poorest schools across the nation.

Returning now to the assertion that students will become more educated and better citizens as a result of the integration of technology into schools, let me note that I have not found any evidence to support this claim. What *is* quite obvious from a review of the research is that the use of technology cannot replace face-to-face communication and that the latter plays a central role in learning (Schofield and Davidson 2002, 312). My discussions with colleagues who use computers in their courses, as well as my own experience, confirm this view. Though I am by no means a computer expert, I do use various software programs such as Blackboard to support my classes. Currently, I am even teaching an online course in the

"Social and Philosophical Foundations of Education," a course designed primarily for students who spend a semester abroad. The experience of teaching this course has taught me that e-mail, discussion boards, and even an audio visual presentation summarizing the main concepts of the readings cannot replace the face-to-face interaction with students. In fact, my experience indicates that there may very well be some concepts that students taking online courses are misunderstanding or failing to grasp because they do not have the benefit of meeting with their instructor, discussing, and asking questions on a regular basis.

Moreover, Armstrong and Casement contend that when children are exposed to computer technology they are not just learning a skill and that using computers alters their relationship to themselves and the world around them. That is, computers shape children's perceptions of knowing and doing in a way that is radically different from more traditional print sources. Armstrong and Casement (2000, 11-12) explain that

> unlike print, which encourages reflection and a careful consideration of various points of view, computer software urges immediate action. Words and images on-screen invite constant change or substitution — this is, after all, one of the things the computer and the software it runs are designed to do. And the faster you can manipulate what you see on the screen, the more control you appear to have over the technology you are using. Speed and control are emphasized at the expense of thoughtfulness and understanding.

To be sure, not all books and articles encourage reflection and questioning; nor is it the case that every computer software program discourages higher order thinking. Still, generally speaking, it is true that print sources promote much more critical analysis and understanding than computer technologies. As Cuban (2001, 189) insists, "the thrill of retrieving hard-to-get information quickly is a long stretch from thoughtfully considering the information and turning it into knowledge or, in time, forging that knowledge into wisdom." If this is the case, then it is clear that the claim that using computers helps students become more educated and better citizens does not hold up. What is at stake here is no less than the ability to think critically and deeply about important issues and consider multiple points of view. These abilities are the hallmark of being an education person and citizen and it is plain that computer technologies are not designed to foster these goals. It is not a stretch to argue that television shows, video games, and many computer software programs, far from helping students become more informed and better thinkers, are actually making them more passive and stupid.

Besides, since computers provide us primarily with visual images, they represent a very narrow conception of the world in which we live and interact with others. This world, as Armstrong and Casement observe, includes not only sights but also sounds, smells, tastes, and textures. They correctly maintain that young children in particular need to be oriented to the world around them in all its complexity and sensual richness:

> Computers cannot provide these kinds of sensory experiences, nor can they cultivate the emotional and intellectual bonds that develop between children and those who help them learn. Computers cannot match a good teacher's ability to inspire interest and excitement in learning. They cannot speak with passion and commitment about ideas. Although a computer program may post a word or two of praise when a child gives a correct answer, the computer does not *care* whether the answer is right or not. It knows when a child has made a mistake, but it is not interested in *why* the mistake has been made. (Armstrong and Casement 2000, 12)

Ultimately, we are shortchanging our children's education when we substitute computer training for the opportunity to learn literature and history in depth, to participate in art and music programs, and to engage in daily physical activity. In putting so much stock in preparing students for a technical world and a global economy, we are compromising some of their most basic physical, emotional, and intellectual needs. Such needs are best met not by getting teachers and students to spend more time with computers in their classes but by ensuring that all children have the opportunity to establish close connections with their teachers. Armstrong and Casement are right when they say that nothing is more important for children's education than the existence of such relationships. Teachers are the ones who can ignite children's curiosity and their interest in exploring questions in science, math, history, and art. "They are not just concerned with *what* their students learn but with *why* they should know about certain things and *how* this knowledge can make a difference to them" (Armstrong and Casement 2000, 202). Only the presence of caring teachers can encourage students to engage in thoughtful exploration and ask the kinds of questions that enhance their learning and development.

Conclusion

This chapter has attempted to sift through some of the rhetoric regarding the integration of computer technologies into schools and classrooms. My analysis suggests that there are a number of myths and falsehoods being disseminated about the use of this technology. To begin with, it is a false belief that the increased availability of technology in schools would result in extensive use. The existing research clearly indicates that, for the most part, the use of computer technology in schools has been limited rather than widespread. Furthermore, contrary to some popular misconceptions, the increased availability and use of this technology has not resulted in higher student achievement on standardized tests or in better teaching and learning practices. One reason why this is true is because most teachers who integrate computers into their teaching do so to maintain their existing practices rather than to make fundamental changes in them. Finally, there is no credible evidence to support the claim that students are becoming more educated and better citizens because of the integration of technology into schools. On the contrary, there is a growing concern that the increased use of computers will result in our children becoming less educated and thoughtful, since computers provide users with a very narrow image of reality and can undermine their ability to think deeply about important issues.

These findings suggest that teachers, administrators, policymakers, and educators in general need to be very cautious and sensible about the push to integrate computer and information technologies into schools. Educators need to be cautious not only because there are many unanswered questions about the use of technology but also because, to date, we have not paid much attention to the limitations of computers as instructional tools. To assume that computers have only advantages and no drawbacks contradicts over 20 years of research on this topic. It indicates an unwillingness to face up to what we have known about teaching, learning, and technology for years now. Viewing technology as a cure for our nation's educational failures disregards the fact that it is, above all, good teachers, not computers, who can make a difference in our children's education.

Chapter Seven

Good Techniques Are Those that Seem to "Work"

In Chapter Four I pointed to the fact that one of the side effects of the growing connections between business and education in the United States is that concepts and models that were originally constructed in the field of business are being applied to education without much serious discussion. For example, in *Shaping School Culture: The Heart of Leadership* Terrence Deal and Kent Peterson note that there is a shared consensus, which they happen to agree with, that schools should behave more like businesses (Deal and Peterson 1999, 10). Yet they never bother to justify this claim, suggesting only that it is plausible to assume that educational improvement will depend on our ability to cultivate the kind of culture in our nation's public schools that has worked to distinguish successful businesses. Packaging their argument in words such as passion, meaning, and commitment, they nevertheless draw on the examples of Starbucks and the Marine Corps to illustrate how large organizations like schools can flourish.

Of course, it may be true that there are some lessons that can be learned on how to improve our schools from the experiences of successful businesses, such as giving teachers more autonomy. Yet, there are a number of good reasons why we should be suspicious of the attempts to reform schools according to the business model, not least of which is the fact that the underlying purpose of schools is very different from that of a successful company. Whether one believes that schools should cultivate individuals who are critical, caring, and creative or

help children become aware of the world around them and their relationship to it, there is little doubt that these goals are not the same as
those that guide thriving businesses. Even if one subscribes to the
much more narrow view that the function of schools is to equip students with the knowledge and skills they need to get by in the world, it
is still true that schools are there to help students learn and not to sell
them knowledge. Simply put, schools are not concerned with making a
profit as businesses are, but with the intellectual, social, emotional, and
moral development of the young.

Moreover, one always has to be extremely careful when attempting
to apply concepts or methods that were created in a particular context
to a completely different set of conditions and circumstances. The reason is that the physical, social, and historical context has a significant
impact on the development of the concepts and methods of the particular discipline being studied. Once the context is altered, the concepts
and methods may have to be changed as well. For instance, B. F. Skinner, one of the founders of Behaviorist Psychology, conducted his early
research on pigeons in the controlled environment of a laboratory. His
concepts of *operant conditioning* and *contingent reinforcement* were originally constructed to explain the behavior of animals in this artificial
context. Later, certain aspects of Skinner's theory were appropriated
into the field of education and particularly classroom management.
Based on Skinner's notion of conditioning, techniques were invented
to manage children's behavior that involved rewarding them for good
behavior and punishing them for bad. However, in the last few decades
the behaviorist approach to learning and classroom management has
been sharply criticized, in large part because it has been recognized
that concepts and methods that may be suited for animals in laborato-
ries are inappropriate to address the problems of children in schools
and classrooms.

In this chapter, I would like to elaborate on the problem of the infiltra-
tion of the concepts and concerns of business into the discourse of
schooling and education, focusing on a different aspect of it. Specifically,
I will target the way in which the appropriation of the language, goals,
and methods of business by many educators is undermining our ability
to address questions of ethics and purpose in education. This problem is
serious for those educators who, like David Brell, believe that the most
important function of schooling is moral education. Brell (2001, 23) is
correct when he writes:

For what could be more important than helping others—and ourselves—to become better people? Even a moment's reflection will reveal that any of the other typically
proffered goals of education (transmission of culture, preparation for the workforce, responsible citizenship) are secondary. They tacitly presuppose that what is learned will be
put to good use — will be used in the service of what is Good
— and that this Good is of higher importance than any of its
subsidiary aims. For there is no higher purpose for our existence than to live a Good life.

IT WORKS, BUT FOR WHAT PURPOSE?

Students in my classes, both pre-service and in-service teachers, frequently raise questions and concerns that suggest that they are looking
for classroom strategies that will work. I often hear comments such as
"we need some techniques that can help us control our classes," or "dividing students by ability really *worked* in my school." When I ask these
teacher candidates to reflect on why it is so important for them to control their students or about the underlying purpose of dividing students into ability groups, many of them acknowledge that they have
not really thought too much about these questions. Basically, they are
sidestepping the question of the educational purpose of the methods
and techniques they value and immediately begin trying to figure out
how they can implement them.

Why is it so important that teacher candidates be required to think
about questions of purpose? Several reasons immediately come to mind.
To begin with is the fact, mentioned in Chapter One, that teaching and
education have been reduced in many public debates and schools to a
technical search to find the most efficient methods to achieve a set of prescribed ends. For instance, the current standards reform initiative is
based on an extremely narrow conception of education in which the
main goal is to prepare children to participate in the global economy. As
Jeff Kane (1998, 3) notes,

> the standards we speak of are not concerned with the needs
> of children, or sense of meaning and purpose in their stud-
> ies, their sense of belonging in community, their sense of
> connection with the world and with others, their sense of
> moral responsibility and the purpose of life itself. The stan-

dards pertain primarily to what information should be in someone's head and how it may be processed to solve a particular problem.

The problem is, as Kane argues, that the issues neglected are *not* peripheral; they are the very essence of a person's education. Unless teacher educators encourage their students to consider questions of purpose, meaning, and morality, many new teachers will come to believe that good teaching involves simply being able to convey information and manage behavioral problems.

Another reason that teachers need to think about the underlying goals of education is that if we agree with Martin Buber's (1955, 104) contention that "education worthy of the name is essentially education of character," then all teachers must view themselves not simply as instructors in a certain body of knowledge or of a particular skill. Rather, they should conceive their task as aiming at the person as a whole, including the moral, spiritual, physical, and affective dimensions of our being, together with the cognitive aspect that most schools focus on. This means that teachers need to be prepared to address the moral dilemmas that arise in the classroom, whether or not they are part of the formal curriculum. For example, social studies high school teachers who are facilitating a discussion on ancient African civilizations in a global history class should, at the very least, raise the following moral questions: What does it mean to be civilized? And how well are the leaders and people of our own society living up to this standard? These teachers should also take into account the emotional impact that a discussion examining the integrity of ancient African civilization will have on minority students in general and on African-American students in particular. If teachers do not pay attention to the moral, psychological, and political dimensions of the learning process, they have little chance of affecting the whole individual, as Buber inspires us to do. Indeed, they may even do damage to their students by presenting an elitist notion of the concept of civilization and a very narrow, exclusively Western view of history.

To be sure, the underlying goals of education should inform everything that goes on in the classroom: how it is organized, what is taught, and what methods are used. This means that the methods and techniques that teachers use to teach a lesson ought to follow directly from the general purpose of that lesson and not the other way around. Not doing so is analogous to a darts player who happens to hit one of the edges of the target and then declares that he was aiming all along for the edge, not the middle. It is to act capriciously and with no reflection, without a clear sense of where one is heading and why. Hence when teacher candidates and new teachers claim that they like certain techniques and activities because they work well in their classrooms, we should immediately stop them and ask for what purpose do they work, for whom, and in what context?

These questions are critical because they call our attention to the notion that good teaching is intentional, not accidental, and that it takes into account individual differences and diverse contexts. Being intentional does not mean that teachers should be inflexible, uncreative, or unwilling to take risks. It means that they ought to have a clear sense of the insights they want their students to attain and be aware that the learning that takes place in their classrooms is not a matter of chance. Considering individual differences and diverse contexts is essential because students do not all learn in the same way or at the same pace and because a lesson that worked well for a specific class in period one may not necessarily work for a different class in period six. Teachers need to keep in mind that not only is each student a unique individual but that each class is different from every other class and that these differences need to impact our teaching.

A couple of years back, I remember observing a fifth grade reading class in an urban elementary school in which a student-teacher was teaching a lesson on poetry. The teacher began the lesson by reading to the class a poem about the moon while the students sat at their desks with their heads down and their eyes closed listening to the poem. When she finished reading the poem, the teacher asked the students to share with the class the kinds of thoughts or feelings the poem evoked in them. Several students raised their hands and voiced a number of different responses like "sadness," "fear," and "a sense of mystery," which were not questioned by the teacher. Next, the teacher played an audiocassette of a man reading this poem and then asked the students the same question about what the poem evoked in them. A number of students contributed thoughts and feelings similar to the ones raised earlier. Once again, the teacher did not attempt to question or "problematize" the students' reactions. Finally, the teacher asked one of the students to read this poem, followed by the same routine of asking the students to share their thoughts and feelings with the class, with a similar uncritical response by the teacher.

As I was observing this half-hour lesson, a question kept entering my mind: What is the underlying purpose of this lesson? Later, when I met with the student-teacher to discuss her lesson, I asked her this question, posing it in different ways. For instance, I asked: "What, in your opinion, was the main goal of this lesson?" or "Why do you think it is so important to teach fifth graders a lesson on poetry?" She replied that this lesson is part of their curriculum and that is why she chose to teach it. When I challenged her to think about the possible underlying goals for a lesson on poetry, she looked at me dumbfounded and acknowledged that no one had previously asked her such questions. Now the point here is certainly not to draw attention to the shortcomings of a particular teacher-candidate, but rather to stress the importance of always keeping our purpose at the forefront of what we are doing in our classrooms. When teachers do not reflect on their underlying purpose, the learning that takes place, if it happens at all, is all too often hollow. For this reason every lesson plan should be informed by the underlying goal that the teacher is aiming for. Otherwise, our lessons are likely to end up like the one described above in which the learning that takes place is neither intentional nor of any particular significance. That is, reading, reflecting on, and discussing poetry are merely educational means that are meaningful to the extent that they can foster goals such as students' creativity, individual expression, and thinking. Without being directed by such goals, poetry lessons can easily turn into another rote activity that gets students to do something, yet has very little educational value.

THE ACTUAL VERSUS THE DESIRABLE

Teacher-candidates and new teachers routinely do not distinguish between two levels of analysis: the actual and the desirable. By *the actual* I mean that which actually exists in the world, such as a current policy or practice in education. *The desirable*, on the other hand, refers to what *ought* to be; that is, those things that schools and teachers can do to improve education or make it more equitable. For example, when discussing Rousseau's concept of "negative education," which implies creating a space to preserve childhood and protect children from danger and harm, students in my classes typically argue emphatically that "in today's society it is impossible to prevent children from being exposed to vice." Citing examples like seedy advertisements, violent TV programs, and video games, students maintain that it is unrealistic to think that we can protect students from these and other damaging stimuli.

While it is certainly true that children are currently bombarded by many images and messages that negatively affect them and that it is not too difficult for many youngsters to gain access to dangerous substances and devices, these observations beg the question that Rousseau raises (1979). The question that needs to be addressed, on the level that I have called the desirable, is whether we as a society should attempt to create a space in which children are safe, cared for, and protected from being overexposed to stimuli that are harmful to them?[1] Interestingly, when I pose the question to my students in this way, most of them immediately agree with the principle that efforts should be made to establish and maintain such a space. Yet, Rousseau's question is seldom raised, let alone seriously considered.

To illustrate this point with a more benign example, let's look at a fairly recent phenomenon: the proliferation of programs and methods that attempt to teach pre-school children everything from basic math to a second language and from reading to computer skills. In recent years, it seems as though new programs like these are introduced into the market almost every other day. Despite the many differences among programs and techniques, all of them accept without question the premise that it is definitely *possible* to teach pre-school-age children these basic skills. Once this assumption is embraced, the only problem that remains is to figure out the most effective and efficient way of teaching the desired skill. However, in focusing almost exclusively on the question of whether these programs can teach young children basic skills, a far more fundamental question is neglected: Is it really desirable to teach pre-school children such skills as opposed to allowing them to discover the world through play?

Moreover, if we accept Brell's position that the most important function of schooling is moral education, educators should seriously weigh the ethical consequences of their actions and practices. Once we begin to assess the moral value of what we do in schools and classrooms, we realize that ethical issues are complex and multifaceted and that we cannot simply rely on prescribed formulas to solve them. School and classroom policies and practices are complex because in education the moral consequences of our actions often come into conflict with practical matters or with other ethical and educational considerations. Thus the question whether a particular practice is desirable frequently cannot be answered in simple yes or no terms.

Take the issue of tracking, which refers to dividing students into different tracks according to ability and interests (e.g., college preparatory, general education, and vocational) and providing each track with separate curricula. Commonly used in middle and secondary schools, tracking is favored by some teachers because it reduces heterogeneity, thereby making it easier for them to teach and meet their students' needs. However, most of the research on tracking suggests that "its effect on student achievement is weak and mixed rather than reliably positive" (Good and Brophy 2000, 275). Moreover, this research clearly indicates that tracking has undesirable cognitive, emotional, and social effects, particularly on students in the low-track classes. Good and Brophy (2000, 276) discuss several of these effects, noting that

> compared with their behavior in high-track classes, many teachers in low-track classes are less clear about objectives, introduce content less clearly and completely, make fewer attempts to relate content to students' interests or backgrounds, and are less receptive to student views. Instruction tends to be conceptually simplified and to proceed slowly, with emphasis on rote memory, oral recitation, and low-level work sheets. In contrast, high-track classes study more interesting, complex material, taught at a faster pace and with more enthusiasm.

Another adverse consequence of tracking is that students in the lower-track classes often become alienated from learning and discouraged from trying hard. The segregation into low-status groups contributes to students' deflated sense of confidence and to their lack of motivation to engage in serious academic work. The research on tracking also suggests that tracking assignments tend to be permanent and that there is relatively little movement from one track to another once the initial assignments have been made. In this way, "initial placement into a low track may categorize a student permanently and close off academic and career advancement options" (Good and Brophy 2000, 277).

Finally, one of the most serious problems with tracking is that it minimizes the interaction among students of different achievement. Since achievement in the United States and elsewhere is closely correlated to one's race, social class, and ethnicity, tracking, in effect, diminishes the interaction between students of diverse backgrounds. As such, it is an undemocratic practice that "consistently rewards the privileged for their privilege and punishes the marginalized for their marginalization" (Kincheloe, Steinberg, and Villaverde 1999, 3).

This brief discussion of tracking students is meant to illustrate the point that educational practices have serious moral implications that need to be carefully assessed. In the case of tracking, the research is fairly consistent that despite some teachers' preference for this practice, its undesirable cognitive, emotional, and social consequences, primarily for the students in the lower tracks, far outweigh the benefits that tracking may provide for teachers. The former are moral issues because they deal with what is good or harmful for students. The latter are considerations of a more practical nature since they focus on matters of preference and expediency rather than questions of right or wrong. In short, the negative *ethical* outcomes that tracking has for students should play a greater role in our decision whether or not to institute this practice than the relatively modest *practical* rewards that some teachers and students may gain from it.

Still, one might object that tracking students has not only practical but moral benefits as well, since teachers in homogenous classrooms will be able to better meet their students' needs. In this view, helping teachers address their students' needs more consistently is considered a moral argument for tracking. The problem is, first of all, that the research does not really support the claim that teachers in homogenous classrooms do a better job of promoting learning than those in heterogeneous classrooms (Good and Brophy 2000, 276). Second, even if it were true that homogenous classrooms enhance learning, we would still need to balance this with all the negative outcomes of tracking students described above. I would argue that the negative moral concerns are much more important because they consider the ethical dilemma from the position of the disadvantaged groups in society (i.e., the students in the lower tracks), a position that is often ignored or marginalized. Such a perspective should be paramount because it is based on the values of equity, diversity, and social justice.

In many cases, then, teachers and other educators have to weight one set of moral concerns against another, which is not an easy thing to do. In other cases, they may assess the practical advantage of a certain practice or policy against its moral shortcomings. Generally speaking, I would argue that moral considerations should be given more weight than practical matters when we deliberate on educational issues. But why is that so? The reason is that if we accept Brell's contention that the most important function of schooling is moral education, then it follows that we need to put moral considerations above other factors that are more practical in nature. In contrast, if one subscribes to a business conception of education, which claims that schools need to prepare students to compete in the global workforce, then one would probably consider practicality and efficiency above moral values. This is not to say that moral issues normally come into conflict with what is practical; indeed, it is often the case that the two go hand in hand. Yet when there is a conflict between these two sets of considerations, then we need to always refer back to the underlying purpose of education in order to shed light on which set should be given greater weight.

Even if one does not accept the view that schools should be concerned predominantly with moral education, ethical considerations should still play a major role in the decisions that educators make. This is because in education we are dealing with the development and growth of children who are human beings, not objects like tables and chairs. Human beings are unique in that they are able to think and reflect on themselves, the world around them, and their relationship to it. They are also emotional beings who can display a wide range of emotions from love and joy to fear and anger. And human beings from a very young age have the capacity to relate to and empathize with others. If educators wish to help children develop and reach their true potential, including their ability to relate to and cooperate with others, they will need to attend to the moral dimension of what they do in schools and classrooms.

A final reason why educators should attend to the moral dimension of what happens in classrooms is that teachers and administrators are usually not fully aware of the ethical implications of what goes on in their schools. Philip Jackson, Robert Boostrom, and David Hansen (1993) analyze in depth the hidden ethical dimensions of schooling in their important book, *The Moral Life of Schools*. For instance, they consider teachers' facial expressions from a moral perspective, noting that these expressions are significant because they communicate a great deal about the value of what is going on in the classroom:

> Looks of kindness, impatience, good humor, sternness, incredulity, indignation, pity, discouragement, disapproval, delight, admiration, suspicion, disbelief — are all part of a teacher's normal repertoire of expressions that routinely come into play in the course of teaching a lesson or managing

a class activity. All convey a moral outlook of one kind or another on what the class as a whole and its individual members say and do. (Jackson, Boostrom, and Hansen 1993, 30)

In short, teachers' expressions can be seen as a moral commentary on the activity in which teachers and students are engaged — a commentary that is typically implicit rather than explicit. Unless teachers become more aware of the moral dimension of their interaction with students, they may fail to realize much of what is happening in their classrooms and schools. Indeed, they may also be inadvertently engaging in practices that are morally problematic and harmful to students.

HOLISTIC EDUCATION: AN ETHICAL APPROACH TO TEACHING

From all that I have said thus far it should be clear that I believe that the education of all children should be guided by strong moral goals and considerations, that is, by an ethical approach to teaching. In what follows, I would like to outline one ethical approach that is particularly relevant to address many of the problems of education and schooling in the United States: Holistic Education. According to Ron Miller (1997, 79), one of its leading advocates, holistic thinking acknowledges

> that human life has a purpose, a direction, a meaning that transcends our personal egos and our physical and cultural conditioning. Holistic thought accepts the possibility that humanity is connected, in a profound way, to the continuing evolution of life and the universe, and that the energies of this evolution are unfolding within each human soul.

In this worldview, every act of perceiving, thinking about, and relating to one's environment is a spiritual act because it is based on a connection between individuals and the world. By connecting with other individuals or with their surroundings, human beings begin to understand the wholeness and significance of the universe.

Miller (1997, 81) goes on to explain that "a holistic perspective is rooted in an epistemology of wholeness, context, and interconnectedness." That is, holistic thinking rejects not only ways of knowing (epistemologies) that attempt to separate knower from the known but also those that are based on a mechanistic worldview in which the only things that count as real are physical objects that can be properly quantified. For example, the Behaviorist approach to psychology asserts that only things that can be accurately measured, like violent behavior, have scientific validity whereas things that pertain to the human psyche, such as emotions, cannot be considered actual data in research. In contrast, holistic thinking insists that the world is far more complex and meaningful than that which is allowed by reductionistic worldviews like Behaviorism. To really understand human beings and their interactions with others, we need to consider their actions from a broad perspective that takes into account the entire range of aspects of our existence (including the cognitive, emotional, physical, and spiritual).

Moreover, holistic thinking asserts that all phenomena "are meaningful, and hence most fully knowable, in terms of contexts that hold their relationships to other phenomena" (Miller 1997, 81). From this perspective, nothing exists in isolation and, therefore, in order to make sense of phenomena or events in the world, we need to examine their relationships to other phenomena or events that help give them meaning. For instance, one cannot begin to comprehend the plight of African Americans in the United States today without considering their present situation in light of major events in the past such as slavery and Jim Crow. Unlike reductionism, which dissects things into component parts, holistic perspectives maintain that to fully understand phenomena we need to view them in their relations to other phenomena.

What are the implications for education and teaching that can be gleaned from the holistic approach? To answer this question, it is helpful to look at some of the main differences between holistic education and more conventional approaches. Miller (1997, 80) points out correctly that

> treating education as a spiritual endeavor rather than as the rational, calculated imposition of social discipline is the crucial difference between holistic and conventional education. By dwelling on discrete facts rather than wonders and mysteries, by standardizing learning processes and assessing them quantitatively, by turning children away from their passions and intuitive insights, and in many other ways, modern schooling cuts the child off from knowing the world in its wholeness.

In contrast, educators who embrace a holistic approach encourage their students to explore the world with a sense of wonder, purpose, and meaning. The emphasis on the spiritual dimension of our being implies that learning will focus on inquiry, dialogue, and creativity rather than on the acquisition of isolated bits of information. The processes of inquiry, investigation, and dialogue are intended to help students not merely take in the information they encounter but to reflect on it and interpret its meaning. Such processes will help them discriminate between facts and ideas that are appropriate to address the needs of humanity versus those that may in fact be dangerous to our existence.

In addition, holistic educators acknowledge that students have diverse learning styles, abilities, and interests and that teaching should address their "multiple intelligences." These educators insist that the cognitive dimension is just one aspect of our being and that schools need to educate the whole person. The implication is that teachers need to view "each child as a feeling, aspiring, meaning-seeking individual rather than merely as a machine-like processor of information" (Miller 1997, 83). This insight implies that schools and teachers will need to engage students in activities that promote their emotional, creative, social, and moral growth and not simply focus on cognitive development.

Based on their conviction that human beings are integrally connected with each other and the universe, holistic educators argue that healthy families and communities are necessary for the full development of students as persons. Such an approach "looks closely at the community life of the classroom, the school, and the neighborhood, to see how meaningful relationships between students and these environments can be encouraged" (Miller 1997, 83). Yet holistic education does not stop at the level of the local community for it challenges students to examine their connections to larger social, political, and economic institutions and problems. Like critical pedagogy and other progressive approaches, holistic education insists that education serve democratic purposes; it encourages students to question the laws, norms, and practices of their society.

This last statement brings me to my main argument in this section: Holistic education is informed by a strong ethical approach to teaching. To assert that education should serve democratic purposes implies that schools need to foster citizens who are critical and caring and who will struggle to make their society a more humane community for everyone. Holistic thinkers like David Purpel call upon educators to speak out against injustice, violence, and oppression and to model for their students an ethical way of being in the world. Indeed, holistic education rejects the business concept of schooling that dominates today, a model that is concerned primarily with standardization, obedience to authority, and preparing students to compete in the global economy. Such a conception is not only far too narrow for holistic thinking but also damaging in that it puts economic concerns above moral and spiritual considerations.

The assertion that schools and teachers should educate the whole person is another indication that holistic education is concerned with ethical values and moral development. Holistic approaches recognize that human beings are not one-dimensional but rather an integrated system of cognitive, emotional, physical, social, cultural, spiritual, and moral realities. Although holistic thinkers generally consider this moral reality as part of the spiritual dimension of our being, it is clear that moral development and values must be at the core of holistic approaches to education. For there is no point in talking about the interconnectedness of all phenomena, developing meaningful relationships with others, or caring for the universe, if we do not believe that people have the capacity to act ethically. Likewise, it does not make sense to condemn the business conception of education and its devastating results for our existence, unless we are convinced that education should foster the capacity to act fairly and humanely toward others and the universe.

Holistic thinking is, therefore, based on the assumption that a worthy education has to address moral development and to educate students to relate to the world in an ethical manner. But unlike more traditional approaches that emphasize moral education, holistic thinking is not grounded on any sectarian dogma, on a set of timeless religious laws that cannot be broken. Neither does it rest on a romanticized version of a golden past to which we should strive to return. Instead, holistic education is guided by a vision of a better sense of community in this world, one in which people relate to each other and their environment as whole persons. The commitment to establish such a democratic and spiritual community is a common feature of virtually all the major holistic thinkers and educators. These thinkers and educators insist on educating students to act ethically toward the world out of a deep concern for the welfare of humanity and the universe as a whole.

CONCLUSION

In celebrating techniques, methods, and practices that "work" in schools and classrooms, teacher candidates and new teachers may be unconsciously appropriating goals, concepts, and standards that are suitable for business to the field of education. My analysis has shown that assessing educational issues according to a business model leads to several problems that are detrimental to both teachers and students. To begin with, there is the problem that in focusing on strategies that work in the classroom, educators often ignore the much more vital question of educational purpose. Being clear and explicit about our purpose in teaching is essential, since our underlying goals shape everything that happens in the classroom — from the methods of instruction to the use of space, from the choice of curricula to the interaction with students. My experiences as well as that of other educators suggests that if teachers do not attend to the general purpose of their lessons, the learning that takes place is generally devoid of any significant value.

Another problem with uncritically embracing practices that currently exist and appear to work in schools is that it undermines our ability to confront ethical issues in education. Yet addressing ethical issues is paramount since most educational decisions and practices have serious moral consequences and many teachers and administrators are not really conscious of the moral implications of their actions. Confronting these issues is also essential because the moral development of the young is one of the most important educational goals. Taking seriously issues of purpose and ethics in education implies that educators need to adopt an approach that ensures that teaching and learning will not only be significant for students but also informed by strong moral considerations. Holistic thinking is a particularly promising approach to meet these ends because it based on the convictions that teachers should educate the whole person and that education should serve democratic and humane purposes.

NOTE

1. Rousseau raises this question in Book II of *Emile or On Education*.

Chapter Eight

More Testing Results in Higher Standards

Standards, accountability, high-stakes testing, and assessment in general are hot issues in education today. Although the concern with higher standards and testing is not really new in the United States (Gordon 2003, 28), these issues have become even more focal since the federal No Child Left Behind Act (NCLB) became law in 2001. This law requires each state to expand its testing plan, mandating among other things that every student from the 3rd through the 8th grades will be evaluated annually in reading and math. Advocates of NCLB argue that it will help us determine if students are meeting the standards that educators have set for them, if teachers and schools are preparing students to meet these standards, and what needs to be done to improve the curriculum and instruction. Critics of the law have been vocal in their opposition to the new mandates, charging that the new standardized tests further increase the pressures on teachers to teach to the test. These critics feel that such test-driven instruction results in a pedagogy that is likely to be based on drill and memorization, sacrifices a broad and more complex curriculum, and contributes to the estrangement of many students from learning. At the core of many of the critiques against NCLB and the standards-based initiative is the conviction that the emphasis on high-stakes testing narrows the entire enterprise of education and ultimately puts our democracy in serious danger.

This chapter critically analyzes the increased emphasis on high-stakes testing and the standards initiative that drives it. Specifically, I look at two frequently overlooked misconceptions that are at the basis of current standards-based reforms. The first is that the achievement of high or rigorous standards consists of the acquisition of a set of prescribed ideas, formula, and skills. This conception of high standards is very narrow and technical, puts a premium on quantity over quality, and undermines the most important function of schooling. The second misconception is that the best way to assess the attainment of high standards is by requiring students to demonstrate performance on standardized exams. Basing my argument on the works of scholars such as James Popham, I contend not only that the vast majority of high-stakes tests do not indicate how well teachers are instructing their students but that these assessment instruments actually do more harm than good to children. I conclude this chapter by discussing an alternative way of conceptualizing student and teacher assessment, an approach that is aimed solely at enhancing teaching and learning.

THE MEANING OF HIGH STANDARDS

The No Child Left Behind Act purports to be guided by lofty goals such as narrowing the achievement gap between disadvantaged and minority children and their peers who live in largely white, middle-, and upper-middle class districts. According to an article posted on the U.S. Department of Education's website on stronger accountability and testing for results, the law will not only help close this gap but also "change the culture of America's schools so that they define their success in terms of student achievement and invest in the achievement of every child." Stated in such terms, it is not easy to argue with the mission of the NCLB. The problems emerge when one begins to read further and look at the details of the new mandates and their underlying assumptions.

Consider, for instance, the following statement in support of the NCLB made in the same article:

> The first principle of accountability for results involves the creation of standards in each state for what a child should know and learn in reading and math in grades three through eight. With those standards in place, student progress and achievement will be measured according to state tests designed to match those state standards and given to every child, every year.

Further down in the same article, the authors compare the need to test children on academic knowledge and skills to taking them to the dentist to examine whether or not they have cavities: "We need to test children on their academic knowledge and skills for the same reason

we take them to the dentist to see whether or not they have cavities —
because we need to know."

To be sure, I have nothing against holding students accountable for
standards and I believe that those standards should be rigorous. It is the
nature of the standards that we hold students accountable for that needs
to be questioned. The statements quoted above assume that high standards are technical in nature and entail the acquisition of a set of predetermined skills and data in reading and math. Yet, as Joe Kincheloe
argues, technical standards, measured by one's performance on standardized tests, are grossly inadequate in that they remove the crucial
meaning-making process from students' learning. "Meaning in this context has already been determined by the curriculum makers and is simply imposed on students as a 'done deal' — there is no room for
negotiation about the interpretation of information" (Kincheloe 2001, 4).
Kincheloe's point is not that teachers and students should disregard the
information that has been generated by others; it is that schools should
place less emphasis on the simple acquisition of a set of predigested facts
and much more on the ability to interpret and make sense of ideas and
experiences that students encounter.

Former Secretary of Education Rod Paige is a vocal advocate of the
NCLB. In a 2004 op-ed article that appeared in *The Washington Post*, Paige
wrote that "the days of free money are over. The *No Child Left Behind Act*
says that if you take federal education dollars, we will ask you to be accountable in terms of raising student achievement...." Achievement
here is defined operationally as performance on an annual standardized
test, not as the ability to engage in inquiry, critical thinking, or creative
projects. To be sure, we want all children to be able to read, write, and
solve math problems by the time they graduate from elementary school.
Yet, to assume that the attainment of such skills indicates that the standards we set are rigorous, dodges the crucial question about the nature
and meaning of high standards.

Moreover, Paige's comments do not show any awareness of
Vygotsky's (1978, 85-86) insight that students' achievement and ability
in general are not fixed and cannot be accurately assessed by simply
looking at what they can do on their own at a particular moment in time.
Vygotsky teaches us that children's achievement can vary greatly de-
pending on the situation, and that we need to carefully consider the social context in which they learn and operate in order to determine their
ability. Although Paige cites data indicating that the majority of African

American and Hispanic students are not proficient in reading by their se-
nior year in high school, he does not appear to be too concerned about
the social conditions of these students, which surely contribute to their
poor performance. As Michael Apple (2001, 188) notes,

> the attempt ... to make decisions about public schools and in-
> stitutions of teacher education based only on the hard data of
> standardized test scores represents the dismissal of any type
> of situation-specific and qualitative understanding that is
> grounded in the lived experience of teachers in real schools.

So what do we mean when we talk about high or rigorous standards?
For Theodore Sizer this issue is very complex and multifaceted and
raises a host of other questions. For example, he asks, do rigorous standards imply

> the expression at a given moment — a testing situation, per-
> haps — of certain facts and skills? Or is it estimable quality in
> the use of those facts and skills in some unfamiliar situation?
> Or is it evidence that the mastery of those facts and skills and
> their resourceful use has become a matter of habit for the
> young person? (Sizer 1996, 44).

Sizer correctly points out that most discussions of high standards focus
only on the first of these categories and sometimes on the second. The
third is usually ignored and refers to the development of habits of mind
like the ability to interpret information and consider issues from multiple perspectives. However, I agree with Sizer that the development of
such intellectual habits is a necessary condition for the purpose of cultivating critical and active citizens in a democratic society.

The attainment of rigorous standards, therefore, takes us far beyond
the mere acquisition of information and skills that are characteristic of
the technical and economic standards being promoted by many
policymakers and educational reformers. For Kincheloe, we must aim
for nothing less than "standards of complexity," suggesting that teachers
and students will need to develop the capacity to ask tough questions
about and critically analyze the knowledge that they access. These questions include such issues as who produced the information that is being
used, who benefits from it, and under what circumstances was it produced. Kincheloe (2001, 5) rightly maintains that addressing these questions is a rigorous intellectual challenge that requires people "to

organize information into meaningful constellations by discerning relationships between ostensibly unrelated data."

Unlike technical standards that emphasize only the ability to locate and retrieve information, standards of complexity focus on sophisticated cognitive skills similar to those possessed by highly skilled researchers, artists, physicians, architects, and other experts. These skills include the ability to interpret information, identify tensions or problems in your approach, and synthesize between seemingly conflicting viewpoints. Kincheloe calls our attention to the fact that students who learn to operate like researchers are able to identify the uncertainties and contradictions in a piece of information and understand a variety of contexts that give meaning to this data. As researchers, these students are also be able to explore how individuals in other social-historical contexts have viewed the information and even construct what other observers have not previously seen in the data (Kincheloe 2001, 10).

To further illustrate the difference between low-level technical standards and standards of complexity, consider the case of two high school history teachers introducing their students to the Civil War. The first teacher approaches this topic as if it were a simple and unambiguous event, emphasizing the names of the major players, key dates to remember, and important battles that were fought. For this teacher, there is only one correct interpretation of the causes and purpose of the War, one that the students need to learn and be able replicate on the exam. In contrast, the second teacher approaches the Civil War as a complicated and controversial event that various scholars have interpreted in different ways. This teacher would get her students to research diverse explanations and analyses of the war, weigh the evidence for each interpretation, and come up with their own conclusions. The second teacher would also want her students to be able to relate the Civil War to earlier events, such as slavery, as well as to more contemporary issues like the Civil Rights Movement and the plight of African Americans today.

This brief example shows that teaching to high standards must not aim at getting students to commit unconnected bodies of information to memory but at *understanding* the various relationships between these bodies of information and their significance to the students and to society at large. A pedagogy informed by standards of complexity helps students make sense of the hidden assumptions and structures that shape our understanding of the world around us. "Such a pedagogy is much more respectful of the sanctity of the past, the intelligence of teachers, and the dignity of students as self-directed agents than a curriculum that simply delivers predigested Truths for passive, unengaged students" (Kincheloe 2001, 9). In contrast, by emphasizing narrow technical standards, most of the current curriculum and testing initiatives undermine students' ability to gain a deep understanding of historical events, scientific problems, and the relevance of literary works to students' lives.

WHAT DO STANDARDIZED TESTS TELL US?

A second assumption that is frequently taken for granted rather than critically examined is that standardized tests are instruments that can fairly accurately assess student achievement and how well teachers and schools are promoting student learning. In fact, many teachers and administrators just accept the notion that standardized tests are a good way of evaluating the quality of instruction that their students are receiving. However, after years of researching the nature and impact of high-stakes testing, James Popham concluded that this assumption simply does not hold up. Popham (2001, 42) argues that "despite the widespread practice of using students' scores on standardized achievement tests to measure a school staff's instructional quality, there are three powerful reasons why this application of such tests is mistaken."

The first reason Popham gives for rejecting the use of standardized tests to assess the quality of teaching has to do with teaching/testing mismatches. Comparing the content of elementary curricula in different school districts to that of the leading national standards achievement tests, Popham and other researchers discovered that what is covered in the test may or may not be addressed in the locally approved curriculum. These studies suggest that there are substantial and unacknowledged mismatches between what is tested and what is taught. In Popham's (2001, 43) words, "if you look carefully at what the items in a standardized achievement tests are actually measuring, you'll often find that *half or more of what's tested wasn't even supposed to be taught* in a particular district or state."

What accounts for these enormous mismatches? To begin with is the fact that there are multiple ways of both teaching and testing students on even the most basic skills, such as reading comprehension. Given this fact, it seems pretty obvious that there will be many instances in which a testing technique will not match the teaching approach that was used. This means that students who are assessed in a way that corresponds to the manner in which they were taught are likely to do much better than those who are taught and tested in divergent ways. Moreover, since children's attention spans are limited, test developers always select a sample of items from the entire array of skills and knowledge they regard as important for any grade level. For example, since it is unrealistic to assess *all* of the content that fourth graders covered in language arts and math during the year, creators of tests must make choices about what to test, and frequently these choices will not mesh with the curriculum emphases of a given state or district. According to Popham (2001, 45), these kinds of mismatches typically go undetected "largely because local educators fail to subject national tests to an item-by-item scrutiny." However, he rightly maintains that an item review is essential in order to determine whether or not a given test is suitable to evaluate instruction in a given school setting.

A second reason that standardized achievement tests should not be used to evaluate the quality of teaching and learning in schools is quite ironic: Since these tests are designed to achieve an optimal score-spread, they tend to exclude items that teachers have emphasized and students have mastered. Items that have been mastered by the majority of the students are typically ones that teachers consider very important and have therefore spent a great deal of time teaching. The irony is that such items are often eliminated from the standardized tests because they do not contribute much to the score-spread among students; that is, they are not able to sort students according to aptitude. Popham (2001, 48) sums up this point well:

> Thus, the more important the content, the more likely teachers are to stress it. The more that teachers stress important content, the better that students will do on an item measuring that content. But the better that students do on such an item, the more likely it is that the item will disappear from the test. How fair is it, then, to evaluate a school's staff on the basis of a test that ... fails to include items covering the most important things teachers are trying to teach? And, of course, those important things will typically be the things that teachers have taught well.

The third and perhaps most compelling reason that standardized achievement tests should not be used to judge the quality of students' education is that factors other than instruction contribute to students' performance on these exams. Indeed, Popham illustrates, with the help of numerous examples, that the students' socioeconomic status as well as their inherited academic aptitudes have a significant impact on their performance on achievement tests. Students' socioeconomic status refers to factors such as household income and parental education levels, which in turn are related to a host of opportunities and experiences that can influence a child's response to a test item. For instance, in contrast to children from low income families, those coming from affluent backgrounds typically grow up in homes where standard American English is spoken and cable TV is available. These children are much more likely to encounter the kind of books, magazines, and newspapers that often form the basis of the test items on standardized exams. Hence, it is clear that students who come from affluent homes bring to these tests a huge advantage compared to their peers from lower socioeconomic backgrounds.

Besides socioeconomic status, students' inherited academic aptitude also plays a major role in their performance on standardized tests. Inherited aptitude refers to those talents and abilities that children are born with. Some youngsters are naturally gifted in sports while others are aesthetically inclined. Some are better at dealing with quantitative problems and others are verbally fluent. To be sure, these natural gifts or abilities do not *determine* children's futures but they do influence their relative success or failure in different areas. All of this is fairly obvious and has even become part of the conventional educational discourse, especially since Howard Gardner introduced his theory of multiple intelligences a couple of decades ago. The problem is that test developers have seized on the fact that children are different in their verbal, spatial, and quantitative potentials and have thrown in a number of items that measure these aptitudes.

> These test items appear to be assessing what children should
> have learned in subject areas such as social studies, science, or
> math. But if you analyze carefully what the *cognitive demands*
> of these items are — that is, what those items are really asking
> students to do — you'll discover that the item is fundamen-
> tally measuring the academic potentials that children were
> fortunate or unfortunate to have inherited from their parents:
> inborn word-smarts, number-smarts, and spatial-smarts.
> (Popham 2001, 66)

So why would standardized achievement tests include items that assess inherited academic aptitude? The reason is that such items do a great job of creating what test developers long for: a nice score-spread among students. Of course, tests that are designed to produce an optimal score-spread may be good at sorting students into different tracks or future professions; but they are not a very good indication of the quality of instruction that students are receiving. The fact that many items are included on standardized exams because they help provide a good score-spread should leave us wondering about the real purpose of such tests. After all, if these exams were really meant to assess the quality of teaching and learning in various grades and subjects, we would not be concerned at all if most students answered the items correctly. Indeed, it would be a cause to celebrate since we could infer that students had mastered what they were taught and supposed to be learning.

A final problem with the use of standardized tests to assess the quality of teaching and learning needs to be mentioned here: There is a huge contradiction between the insistence on a constructivist approach as the best way to promote student learning and the use of standardized testing to assess children's understanding of academic content. A constructivist approach to teaching asserts that learning is most significant when students are active participants in the process of interpretation and construction of knowledge rather than merely sponges expected to absorb the information produced by teachers. In many states across the country, teachers are being evaluated on their ability to promote active and successful student participation in the learning process, their skill in varying instructional strategies to account for different learning styles, fostering higher order thinking skills, and using authentic methods of assessment. However, at the end of the year, a standardized test is used to assess their students' mastery of the statewide curriculum. Martha Casas (2003, 3) highlights this contradiction well:

> Sitting for two or three hours selecting correct answers to a series of reading and mathematics questions with some restroom breaks in between is a contradiction to how children learn each day. During testing the children cannot ask their teachers or their classmates for help in taking the test. Yet, in their daily routines teachers offer students their help to understand challenging work, and students often work collectively in problem-solving activities.... Assessment needs to be a natural part of the learning process. Having children's daily routines interrupted for taking a test that is measuring

concepts that the students might not be learning that week
defeats the purpose of authentic assessment.

All of the evidence presented above leads me to conclude that the current standardized achievement tests are tools that should never be used to assess the value of schooling that students are getting. This is not to suggest that it is impossible to create tests that help teachers promote student mastery of important skills and knowledge and provide us with credible evidence about the quality of our nation's schools. The point is that most of the tests that are used today do more harm than good since the information they supply about the quality of schooling is completely unreliable. In addition, as mentioned above, high-stakes testing programs lead to pressures on educators to raise test scores, pedagogical practices based on drill and memorization, a narrowing of the school curriculum, and the misidentification of inferior and superior schools (Popham 2001, 17). In the face of all the evidence of serious problems with the content and application of standardized tests, it is outrageous that current educational policymakers are calling for their increased use.

RETHINKING ASSESSMENT

There is a well-known anecdote attributed to Albert Einstein, in which he was asked by a reporter if he knew his mother's phone number. Einstein responded that "I do not remember the number, but I know how to find it." This brief anecdote illustrates the difference between traditional conceptions of assessment and the alternative notion that I am advocating here. Traditional testing assumes that knowledge of a topic means the ability to exhibit certain facts and skills at a particular moment in time. In this case, teaching is aimed at covering the material that will be included on the exam and since the amount of information to be learned is usually immense, deep understanding of the issues cannot help but be sacrificed. I still remember some of my own high school classes in which teachers would spend many lessons dictating the information to us that we needed to remember for the matriculation exam at the end of the year. Many of us could barely keep up with the pace of dictation, let alone pause for a moment to reflect on what we were writing down.

In contrast to most standardized tests that measure the *quantity* of information that the students have learned, genuine assessment has to focus on the *quality* of understanding and the ability to engage in deep thinking and inquiry. This is why it is insignificant that Einstein could not remember his mother's phone number. What matters is that he knew how to get it when needed; that is, he was aware of how to approach and investigate this problem. Unlike standardized testing that forces students to de-contextualize their knowledge and skills, the alternative conception of assessment proposed here enables students to engage with problems that are connected to real-life situations. Referred to by various names such as performance-based assessment, authentic assessment, and exhibitions, these tests require students to think deeply and creatively about issues that matter to them, research the issues, and demonstrate their knowledge of them to others. Peter Sacks (1999, 257), who has studied this topic extensively, illustrates some of the advantages of this alternative approach to testing:

> By putting context over abstractness, understanding over recollection, process over the bottom line, and performing over filling in Number 2 pencil bubbles, teachers who have used the new assessments have demonstrated an uncanny ability to engage students in learning, indeed, to instill a love of learning and a continuing desire to learn.

Performance-based assessments are usually theme-based, often integrating different disciplines together, and requiring students to demonstrate their work over a period of time. Ted Sizer describes an example of a high school humanities performance-based task (which he calls "Exhibitions"), in which students are asked to explore, analyze, and report on the concept of slavery. In this example, students are asked to create a portfolio of images of slavery that includes the perspectives of both slaves and masters, analyze these images, and come to conclusions about the impact of the institution of slavery for African Americans today. The students would then be required to present their work to their teachers and peers and discuss their ideas and conclusions with others. As Sizer (1996, 84) puts it, "with Exhibitions, the students must expect to be challenged. They have to able to display their knowledge and explain it. They have to understand the material well enough to respond to questions that probe that understanding."

Another example of a performance-based task, suitable for middle or high school science and math classes, focuses on the problem of environmental waste. The task, titled Green Groceries, asks students to address the following challenge:

As an environmentally conscious grocery store chain with a
112 stores in the Southeast, the Green Groceries Company
wanted to design a twelve-ounce cylindrical container for an
herbal soft drink that would minimize the amount of waste in
production. The students — market researchers for the company — were to report their findings to their supervisors in
the marketing department. (Sacks 2000, 239)

The students' challenge is to design the package, write a report about
their product, and produce a video commercial that would market their
company and the new product. Sacks maintains that the students are assessed on all their work, including the design, the written report, the
commercial as well as how well they work together in teams.

These two examples of performance-based tasks illustrate, first of all,
that for students to achieve rigorous standards — the type of standards
described at the beginning of this chapter — the challenges that we use to
assess them must be difficult and complex. To construct a well-thought-
out argument and to be prepared to defend it in front of others is no easy
task. Neither is it simple to design a product that meets certain efficiency
requirements and be able to convince people that this product is better
than the competition. Such tasks are much more complex and difficult
than the memorization and application of facts, dates, and formulas that
students are required to do on most standardized exams. Indeed, it is absolutely essential to require students to take on such challenges because
they force students to think, to use their imaginations and creativity, and
because they prepare students for the kinds of challenges they will face
as adults in their careers and in their relations with others.

Moreover, performance-based assessment, as its name indicates, focuses on students' performance, that is, on their learning and development. Unlike standardized achievement tests that frequently measure
students' inherent academic potential, performance-based assessments
evaluate what students have actually learned and are able to do. When
the focus of testing shifts from sorting and tracking students to assessing
their learning and development, the question becomes not who has met
the standard and who has not, but how can we help students who are not
learning do better. Likewise, if teacher evaluation was aimed chiefly at
helping people become better teachers, then practices like the one described in Chapter One, in which teacher-candidates were encouraged
by their colleagues to repeat a lesson they had already taught when their

supervisor visited their classes, would not happen. In short, performance-based testing rests on the assumption that the primary purpose of assessment is not to compare scores, sort, or punish students, but to improve the quality of teaching and learning.

Research shows that when teachers get students involved in projects and use performance-based assessments to evaluate their learning, remarkable things can happen. Particularly for students who are bored in school and do not see the relevance of schoolwork to their aspirations and circumstances, the changes that occur are quite dramatic. For instance, in 1997, Ann Hayes, a veteran teacher with a great deal of special education experience, was placed in charge of an experimental class of fifteen "at risk" students. The kids in Hayes's class found it very difficult to get excited about math; they could not see how algebra had anything to do with what they will end up doing in life. Realizing that she had nothing to lose, Hayes decided to launch the Green Groceries project with her students. Once her students realized that the project was real and that it was their challenge to figure it out, a huge transformation occurred.

> They *wanted* to solve the problem of creating a can for an herbal drink that would conserve raw materials; and they understood the importance of presenting their findings as professionally as they could and persuading their audience of their solution's feasibility. Hayes' pupils immersed themselves in requisite lessons and exercises in geometry, algebra, writing, and other subjects because those lessons took on new meaning. Suddenly, all that boring stuff became necessary tools to complete the project. (Sacks 2000, 240)

But what would happen to test scores and accountability if more schools were to implement thematic instruction, projects-based learning, and authentic assessment? Conventional wisdom suggests that the more teachers directly prepare students for the exams, going over facts and formulas that are likely to be covered on the standardized tests, the better students would perform on them. The implication is that students who are required to engage in extensive projects and performances to evaluate their learning will not do as well as those who spend most of their time studying for these tests. However, the research that I have looked at indicates that, for the most part, just the opposite happens (e.g., Sacks 2000, 242-243). In fact, students who are involved in projects on serious academic issues have been shown to do very well on standardized exams.

Actually, this finding makes sense when we remember that projects and performance-based assessments help students gain a deeper understanding of the subject. That this understanding would lead to a good performance on a standardized exam should not surprise us all that much.

Still, states, districts, schools, and even individual teachers inevitably have to make choices about what and how to teach students. Based on the discussion above, it should be clear that students would be much better served if they had the opportunity to engage in projects that are both challenging and significant to them. In order to make this a reality, there is no doubt that we would have to reverse the current trend of forcing students to take more and more tests each year. The enormous amount of time used by teachers to prepare students for these exams, not to mention the time spent on the tests themselves, takes away valuable time that could be better spent on projects and performances. Reducing the number of standardized tests that students are required to take will also help educators focus their efforts on the most important function of schooling: ensuring that all students are provided with the kind of experiences that enable them to learn and develop. Such an initiative will help us remember that the process and quality of learning are much more important than a score on any state or national test.

In addition, experience suggests that in order to achieve rigorous academic standards, *less is more*. In other words, it is far better to study a few topics in depth and understand them well than to cover many subjects in a cursory manner. High-stakes testing and the standards initiative that drives it encourage a type of learning that is based on the sweeping coverage of important issues and, thus, never gets beyond a surface treatment of subject matter. Sizer emphasizes that such an approach leads students to develop the habit of learning superficially, a habit that once learned is very difficult to change. In contrast, students who have learned how to explore a topic in depth, in all its complexity, and have been required to demonstrate this knowledge in some kind of performance-based assessment, are much more likely to demand high standards of themselves later in life.

CONCLUSION

Contrary to much of the rhetoric on assessment that is being produced today, this chapter has demonstrated that there are a host of problems associated with the claim that more testing will lead to higher standards. First is the false notion that high or rigorous standards are technical in nature and involve the acquisition of a set of prescribed skills and information in the different disciplines. Actually, rigorous standards are not technical at all and refer to a host of complex cognitive skills similar to the ones possessed by expert scholars, researchers, practitioners, and artists. Given this alternative notion of high standards, the next question that was addressed is whether or not standardized tests are a good way of assessing them. Clearly, the kinds of standardized achievement tests that dominate the educational system today do not even begin to measure the sophisticated cognitive skills that we would want all educated citizens to possess. More troubling, however, is the fact that most of the high-stakes tests are seriously flawed and cannot be used to evaluate the quality of students' schooling. In fact, these assessment instruments lead to a host of negative consequences for both students and teachers. Hence, it is essential to devise alternative ways of conceptualizing assessment, like the one proposed here, that do not share the problems of current standardized tests and are able to give us a good indication of the quality of instruction and learning in our nation's schools.

Chapter Nine

Multicultural Education

It's Only About
Heroes and Holidays

In fourteen hundred and ninety two
Columbus sailed the ocean blue.
It was a courageous thing to do,
But someone else was already here.[1]

A few years ago, when my daughter was a kindergarten student in one of the local public schools in White Plains, New York, she came home one day in mid-October reciting the famous rhyme: "Columbus sailed the ocean blue, in fourteen hundred and ninety-two." White Plains is a diverse community of about 50,000 people, including many African Americans and Hispanics, many of which are immigrants from countries like Haiti, Mexico, Peru, and the Dominican Republic. Disturbed by the thought that what children were learning about Columbus was not very different from what I had received in elementary school more than thirty years earlier, I questioned my daughter about what her teacher had said about the man. Her response was rather bland and common, recalling only that he was that poor European who discovered the New World.

Wanting to find out more information about how Columbus and his conquests were being taught at the end of the second millennia, I decided to attend a monthly meeting of parents, teachers, and administrators in my daughter's school. Although these meetings were devoted to dealing with more "burning" issues, such as testing and planning the school's enrichment programs, I managed to squeeze in a simple question reflecting my concern: "Does the district or school have a policy re-

garding how to address controversial issues?" I think it was the principal
who responded that "there is no such policy, but we are certainly open to
considering multiple perspectives." From here the discussion quickly
moved on to the next item on the agenda, which had to do with planning
for the science fair.

The following year, my daughter, who was now in first grade, re-
turned from school one day in mid-October singing the same rhyme.
This time I decided to go speak to her teacher, believing that maybe she
would be more interested in and open to listening to my concerns about
this issue. So one afternoon, when I came to pick up my daughter from
school, I ran into her teacher in the hall and tried to gently broach this
topic with her. "I was just wondering, what the kids in your class are
learning about Columbus this year?" She paused for a moment and then
muttered something about the busy schedule and the sensitive subject.
"I guess I just try to teach them some basic facts about this explorer and
his journey to the new world," she said. "At the same time," I replied, "I
think it is important that even first graders are exposed to more than one
side of this story." "Yes," she said and reminded me as she hurried off
that my daughter was doing great in school. Driving back home that day,
I remember thinking that it is not a stretch to suppose that many of the
descendents of the same people that the conquistadores had plundered
and enslaved are now, after immigrating to the United States, forced to
sing Columbus's praises. The bitter irony of five- and six-year-old children extolling every October the deeds of the man who oppressed their
ancestors stayed with me for a long time.

This true anecdote highlights a problem with the way in which history in general and heroes and holidays in particular are taught in our
public schools. Much like my daughter's experience with Columbus,
these topics are generally addressed in a way that eliminates all controversy, ambiguity, and conflict. According to James Loewen (1996) who
conducted a monumental study of history textbooks, these books encourage students to believe that history is just facts to be learned, devoid
of any serious debate, clashes of opinions, and opposing values. Yet, as
James Baldwin (1963) eloquently reminds us, "American history is longer, larger, more various, more beautiful and more terrible than anything
anyone has ever said about it." What makes our history at once beautiful
and terrible, fascinating and repulsive are precisely the controversies,
conflicts, debates, and struggles that are generally eliminated from history textbooks and lessons.

In the same way, most teachers and schools reduce multicultural education to an acknowledgment and appreciation of the holidays, traditions, and heroes of different cultures and religions. That is, multicultural education is frequently interpreted in a politically correct manner that seeks to expose students to the worthy contributions of various cultures in order to get them to become more tolerant of differences and respectful of other people. Indeed, according to Sonia Nieto (2000, 303), "when multicultural education is mentioned, many people first think of lessons in human relations and sensitivity training, units about ethnic holidays, education in inner-city schools, or food festivals." Such a view of multicultural education is not only a complete watering down of this concept but also reflects a profound misconception about its meaning and purpose.

THE PROBLEM

But what is wrong with regarding multicultural education as simply the acknowledgment and appreciation of diverse cultures and traditions? After all, for generations this approach to education did not exist in American schools and there was relatively little awareness that such an approach was even needed. Isn't a limited conception of multicultural education better than not addressing this issue at all? In short, don't we make our children better people and improve our society when we recognize cultural differences and celebrate those differences? In order to adequately respond to these questions we must first look more closely at two vital issues that are at the basis of multicultural education: the structure of our society and the purpose of education.

THE STRUCTURE OF SOCIETY

By the "the structure of society" I mean how American society is constructed and organized economically, socially, legally, and politically. Examining these economic, social, legal, and political structures immediately calls our attention to the issues of power and wealth and to the ways in which power and wealth are unequally distributed in this country. Moreover, to truly understand these structures we must look at the United States and its different races and ethnic groups from a broad historical perspective. And any honest historical investigation of this country from the time of Columbus to the creation of the American Republic and from the African slave trade through the Civil War up to the present must arrive at the conclusion that this history is not pretty.

Take the issue of racism, for instance, and specifically racism against African Americans in this country. James Loewen has vividly documented how even though today's history textbooks discuss the slavery of African Americans and its impact on blacks, they generally ignore the racism instituted by white Americans that was largely responsible for slavery. Indeed, Loewen rightly suggests that for the most part the teaching of history in public schools marginalizes racism in American history and even makes it invisible. The reality, however, is that it is impossible to understand the institution of slavery as a major event in our history, whose lingering legacy still haunts many African Americans, without confronting the issues of racism and white supremacy. For Loewen (1996, 144),

> the very essence of what we have inherited from slavery is the idea that it is appropriate, even "natural," for whites to be on top, blacks on the bottom. In its core our culture tells us — tells all of us, including African Americans — that Europe's domination of the world came about because Europeans were smarter.

Equally significant is the problem that by making racism invisible in history textbooks and lessons, we encourage students to believe that race relations have been steadily improving on their own and that racism and discrimination are no longer serious problems in our society. The truth, however, is that racial segregation and discrimination are alive and well in this country, most notably in our public schools as evidenced by Jonathan Kozol's (1992) study of numerous disadvantaged schools across the country. In addition, massive racial disparities remain in such key areas as income, career opportunities, and life expectancy. For instance, in 2001, according to the U.S. Census Bureau website, the median family income for whites was $54,067; for blacks the median income was $33,598; and for Hispanics it was $34,490. Earning more money in our society is closely connected to better education, job opportunities, health care, and housing, and, more generally, to a life that is freer from danger and stress.

What accounts for these huge racial disparities between African Americans and Hispanics in the United States as compared to whites? How can we interpret, for example, their lower educational achievement on reading and math tests? The simple explanation offered by some theorists that whites have higher intelligence levels or that non-whites have some cultural deficit is contradicted by numerous studies that indicate that the relationship between achievement and race disappear when certain economic and social factors are controlled. Moreover, if we follow the IQ and the cultural deficit theories to their logical conclusions we should expect to see the largest discrepancy in achievement between white students and students of color before they entered school. In actuality, research shows that this difference increases during the students' tenure in school, suggesting that environmental and social factors rather than innate abilities have the most impact on student learning and achievement (Persell 1977, 2).

An adequate explanation of the achievement gap between whites and students of color must therefore begin by looking history and laws and practices, such as the Jim Crow statutes that were enacted by whites to segregate blacks and seriously curtail their civil and economic rights. As Loewen (1996, 161) notes, especially between 1890 and 1920 white Americans from both the North and South joined hands to terrorize black communities and reduce blacks to the status of second-class citizens. Of course, even before the Civil War whites in many states made it a crime for African Americans to learn how to read and become better educated. Even today, huge discrepancies continue to exist between white middle-class and lower-class, predominantly minority districts in access to funding, resources, and, most importantly, quality teachers. These "savage inequalities," as Kozol has called them, are not a result of bad luck or of poor choices made by people of color. Rather, they are the product of various historical, political, and legal efforts among whites to systematically prevent or restrict the educational development of blacks and others. Thus, as Loewen writes, "without causal historical analysis, these racial disparities are impossible to explain."

Another key issue that high school students as well as younger children are misinformed about is the conquest of the Americas by the Europeans and their relations with the Native Americans who were here before. Loewen has described in some detail how history textbooks and teachers generally downplay the cruelty, destruction, and even genocide that Columbus and other European conquerors wreaked on the Native Americans. Likewise, the teaching of history is silent about the way in which Native Americans were systematically driven from their lands following the creation of the American Republic, about how the natives fought back and resisted these initiatives, and how the United States continuously broke treaties it enacted with the Indians.

Moreover, our students are graduating from public schools with little awareness of how Indian (as well as African) ideas and practices have influenced our shared American culture past and present. They leave school without gaining even a basic understanding of the extent to which the American society and our ways of life have always been multicultural. This is in large part because there is almost no mention in history textbooks and lessons of how Native American traditions were, at least in part, one of the sources of our democratic institutions, farming practices, foods, names, and other cultural artifacts. Acknowledging these important contributions to our culture would require us to reevaluate the racist assumption that the native population of America was not as civilized as the European colonists who immigrated here some 400 years ago. In Loewen's (1996, 113) words,

> if we recognized American Indians as important intellectual antecedents of our political structure, we would have to acknowledge that acculturation has been a *two*-way street, and we might have to reassess the assumption of primitive Indian culture that legitimates the entire conquest.

This brief sketch of the relations between whites and African Americans and Native Americans is not meant as a history lesson but merely as an illustration that the United States was established from the very outset on a political, legal, economic, and social structure that was fundamentally one-sided. This structure was designed to make sure that wealthy and middle-class white Americans could get the kind of benefits that enable them to develop and thrive financially, educationally, and socially. At the same time, the same structure ensured that African Americans, Native Americans, minorities, and the poor would remain as the underclass and could therefore never achieve the same material, educational, political, and social benefits as middle and upper-class whites. Despite the changes that came about as a result of the Civil Rights Movement, American society remains unfair and undemocratic even today, preventing African Americans and other people of color from getting the same kind of privileges and benefits as whites. Understanding the way in which the United States is constructed and organized is essential in order to bring about any kind of meaningful change to this unjust system of power.

To be sure, one can be aware of the grim realities of American history and still deny that this history has an impact on the opportunities and achievements of different races, ethnic groups, and classes. According to Gary Howard (in Banks 1996, 327) , this attitude of denial is very common among many white Americans who claim that

> the past doesn't matter. All the talk about multicultural education and revising history from different cultural perspectives is merely ethnic cheerleading. My people made it and so can yours. It's an even playing field and everybody has the same opportunities, so let's get on with the game and quit complaining. We've heard enough of your victim's history.

For Howard, this denial is harmful not only because it suggests an unwillingness to face up to the truth but also because it is based on a deep fear of diversity. It would seem, therefore, that education has a key role to play in helping students come to terms with the ugly realities of the past and to confront their fear of diversity.

THE ROLE OF EDUCATION

Given the unequal power structure that exists in the United States that benefits some races and classes and hurts others, what is the role of education? Historically, the education system in this country as well as in other democracies has for the most part been traditional; that is, it has functioned as an instrument of the government to maintain the status quo. Loewen's research illustrates that by feeding students a huge amount of insignificant and isolated facts, history textbooks and lessons attempt to get them to become proud and obedient Americans, content not to ask too many questions and think critically. Such an approach to education attempts to get students to adapt to the political, social, and economic situation that exists, unfair though it may be, rather than seek to change it.

In stark contrast to the traditional model of education, Critical Pedagogy is an approach that attempts to empower students to become more deeply aware of the various problems that affect their lives, problems that are related to larger social, political, economic, and moral issues. The advantage of focusing on problems rather than mere facts, as happens in traditional education, is that students will gain a critical awareness of themselves in relation to the world. Such an awareness will hopefully lead students to become committed to changing those oppressive and undemocratic laws, institutions, and practices.

Informed by the insights of thinkers like Paulo Freire, Critical Pedagogy is aimed at liberating the disadvantaged groups in each society from their bondage and empowering their members so that they will be able to live decent, humane lives. The kind of empowerment that Freire has in mind is a radical one, one that nourishes the capacity of the oppressed to both understand and transform their world. Although Freire first developed his pedagogical approach at the end of the 1960s in the context of the poor and illiterates of northeastern Brazil, his educational insights are particularly relevant for the problems of the disadvantaged in this country. As Richard Shaull argues in the Foreword to *Pedagogy of the Oppressed* (Friere 1994), the educational philosophy and methodology that Freire developed may be as important for addressing the problems of education in the United States as they are for helping the dispossessed of Latin America:

> Their struggle to become free subjects and to participate in
> the transformation of their society is similar, in many ways,
> to the struggle not only of blacks and Mexican Americans
> but also of middle class young people in this country. And
> the sharpness and intensity of that struggle in the develop-
> ing world may well provide us with new insight, new mod-
> els, and a new hope as we face our own situation. (Freire
> 1994, 11)

My contention is that Critical Pedagogy is an educational approach that is particularly useful in addressing problems such as the inequality, poverty, racism, and discrimination that plague our society. The reason that Critical Pedagogy is so helpful in getting students to understand and confront these problems is that it considers the world from the vantage point of the powerless, a perspective that is typically marginalized or ignored. Such a perspective is invaluable not only because it enables us to genuinely understand the plight of the dispossessed in their own voices, but also because it is based on the democratic principles of freedom, equality, and social justice. Unlike more traditional approaches to teaching that seek to maintain the existing power relations in society, Critical Pedagogy insists that education must serve democratic and humane purposes. From this perspective, education must *empower students to make changes* in society rather than *condition them to adapt* to it.

A Broad Conception of
Multicultural Education

We are now ready to revisit the question posed earlier whether or not multicultural education should only acknowledge and appreciate diverse cultures and traditions. Based on the discussion above of the structure of society and the role of education, it is clear that this narrow and limited view of multicultural education is not adequate. Specifically, in light of the argument that the United States was established on a foundation of an undemocratic and unfair power structure that continues to flourish today, a true conception of multicultural education will need to acknowledge this serious problem and attempt to correct it. We cannot pretend to support multiculturalism by celebrating cultural diversity and having food festivals, while we continue to operate in political, economic, and educational systems that perpetuates inequality and discrimination. If we truly believe that the role of education is to get students to become more aware of and respond to the inequalities that exist in their communities, then we should reject the feel-good approach to multicultural education and replace it with a broader approach that can empower students to bring about social transformation.

A broadly conceptualized perspective on multicultural education must, therefore, confront the various forms of inequality and discrimination that exist in our society and work vigorously to change them. According to James and Cherry Banks (1997, 435), multicultural education is

> a reform movement designed to change the total educational environment so that students from diverse racial and ethnic groups, both gender groups, exceptional students, and students from each social class group will experience equal educational opportunities in school, colleges, and universities. A major assumption of multicultural education is that some students, because of their particular racial, ethnic, gender, and cultural characteristics, have a better chance to succeed in educational institutions *as they are currently structured* then do students who belong to other groups or who have different cultural and gender characteristics. (Emphasis added)

A key component of this definition is the assumption that some students have a better chance than others to succeed in our educational institutions as they are currently structured. The point is that the achievement gap mentioned above between white middle-class students and students of color should not be attributed to certain characteristics of the lower achieving students, but rather to the differential opportunities and treatment that students receive once they arrive in school. For instance, research shows that the achievement gap is increased by factors such as school resources, teacher attitudes, and biased testing. Yet, according to Geneva Gay (in Banks and Banks 1997, 213),

> too many teachers still believe that students of color are either culturally deprived and should be remediated by using middle-class Whites as the appropriate norm, or do not have the aspirations or capacities to learns as well as European Americans.

These teachers cling to the misguided notion that the students themselves, not the way they are regarded and treated, are to blame for their poor performance in school.

Banks and Banks' definition also makes it clear that multicultural education should not be reduced to what James Banks calls "content integration," which is the infusion of content related to various ethnic and cultural groups into the curriculum. Conceptualizing multicultural education in this way is problematic for several reasons. First, content integration usually does not get much beyond tokenism, or the inclusion of mere representative examples of different ethnic and cultural groups. Students in high school may read Toni Morrison's *Beloved* and Sandra Cisneros's *The House on Mango Street*; they may celebrate Black History Month and the International Women's Rights Day. Yet such tokenism rarely leads to an in-depth study of diverse races, genders, and cultures and it usually does little more than depict the different groups as *other* than the norm.

Second, since a multicultural content is easier to connect to disciplines such as language arts and social studies, teachers in other disciplines may dismiss multicultural education as irrelevant to their subject. It is fairly common to hear math and science teachers state that "multicultural education is fine for social studies and literature teachers, but it has nothing to do with me. Math and science are the same, regardless of the culture of the kids" (Banks 1996, 20-21). This attitude is defensible only if we subscribe to an overly narrow definition of multicultural education as content integration and ignore all its other dimensions. If, on the other hand, we broaden the definition of multicultural education to include its connections to Critical Pedagogy and to transforming the entire culture of the school, its relevance to subjects like math and science becomes more obvious. Once educators realize that multicultural education is as much about *how* we teach kids as it is about *what* we teach them, the resistance of math and science teachers to this approach may well decrease.

This last insight should be underlined because many educators fail to recognize that multicultural education needs to move beyond content integration and address the issue of how we teach students and how they learn. Like Critical Pedagogy, multicultural education is based on the assumption that students are not passive consumers of information, but rather active and reflective participants in the learning process. This means that teachers need to conduct their classes and interact with students in ways that are more democratic, and they need to design their lessons to encourage students to express their opinions and become more critical. When teachers give students a voice and show them that they value their opinions, students gain a better understanding of the complexity of the world and the multiple perspectives that give it meaning. The point is that getting students to become more active and critical is just as important in math and science as it is in literature and social studies classes. In science, for example, we want all students to be familiar with a number of theories that explain the origin of the universe, the evidence that supports them, their limitations, as well as the social-historical context in which they were created.

Besides the misleading notion that multicultural education should be reduced to content integration, many educators falsely believe that having a multicultural program in their schools automatically takes care of the problems of discrimination and racism. However, Sonia Nieto rightly insists that a multicultural program that does not address the problems of racism and discrimination head on is deeply flawed. To support her claim, Nieto (2000, 36) cites Meyer Weinberg who argues that

> most multicultural materials deal wholly with the cultural distinctiveness of various groups and little more. Almost never is there any sustained attention to the ugly realities of systematic discrimination against the same group that also happens to utilize quaint clothing, fascinating toys, delightful fairy tales, and delicious food. Responding to racist attacks and defamation is also part of the culture of the group under study.

For Nieto, addressing the problems of racism and discrimination means that educators should focus on all the areas in which some students are favored over others: "the curriculum, choice of materials, sorting policies, and teachers' interactions and relationships with students and their families" (Nieto 2000, 306).

Taking on the ugly realities of racism and discrimination, whether the issue is an historical event such as slavery or a current unequal educational policy, is a dangerous topic for many schools and teachers. To name these issues for what they really are is risky because there is a chance that some students will react strongly or highly defensively. The fear of educators to take on these risks leads to the practice of sanitizing the curriculum in order to eliminate all controversy, ambiguity, and conflict; it also leads to the tendency of teachers to teach a feel-good history that will not offend anyone.

The irony here is that teachers who teach history as though clashes of opinions or struggles between different classes and races did not exist, ultimately end up offending other students, most notably students of color. I remember observing a few years ago a diverse high school history class in Brooklyn in which the teacher was facilitating a discussion on ancient African cultures with the aim of trying to determine if they were "civilized." This particular discussion happened to take place only a few days after the massacre at Columbine High School so I was hoping that the teacher would relate this horrific incident to the topic. When this did not happen I was disappointed, feeling that a genuine opportunity had been missed to engage the students in a discussion about the various meanings of "being civilized." My disappointment was confirmed a few minutes later when the bell rang and two African-American students sitting next to me looked at each other in disbelief and one of them remarked, "Is what happened in Columbine civilized?"

This incident suggests that if we agree with Nieto that multicultural education needs to be explicitly antiracist, teachers will need to expose students to the subject matter in all its complexity, including the parts that are risky and not pretty. Being antiracist also means that teachers, students, and educators in general must work constructively to combat racism. For Nieto (2000, 307), this means

> making antiracism and antidiscrimination explicit parts of
> the curriculum and teaching young people skills in confront-
> ing racism. It also means that we must not isolate or punish

students for naming racism when they see it, but instead respect them for doing so. If developing productive and critical citizens for a democratic society is one of the fundamental goals of public education, antiracist behaviors can help to meet that objective.

To cultivate critical and active citizens, educators will need to abandon the narrow conception of multicultural education and replace it with the broader approach described above. This broader approach recognizes that multicultural education is not a peripheral topic, but one that is fundamental to the core curriculum. I agree with Nieto who argues that developing multicultural literacy is just as important as reading, writing, math, and computer literacy for living in today's world. Multicultural literacy implies, at the very least, that students will become fluent in a second language, familiar with the history and geography of not only the United States but of other countries around the world, and aware of the literary and artistic contributions of different peoples (Nieto 2000, 310). It also implies the development of what Kincheloe and other scholars have called "media literacy," which has to do, among other things, with the ability to detect cultural stereotypes and to recognize how different races, religions, and ethnic groups are represented in the media (Kincheloe and Steinberg 1996, 232-233). If students do not acquire this literacy, there is little chance that they will develop an understanding and appreciation of the diverse interests, cultures, and values that co-exist in this country.

Ultimately, adopting a genuine multicultural approach will require educators to transform the entire culture of the school. As Nieto insists, multicultural education is not just another subject area to be covered or something that happens at a set period of the day like lunch or recess. Limiting multicultural education to a particular period that is taught by a specialist gives the impression that this approach is separate from all other school knowledge. Instead, a true multicultural approach must be widespread and integrated throughout the curriculum and the daily school schedule. According to Nieto (2000, 313),

a true multicultural approach is pervasive. It permeates everything: the school climate, physical environment, curriculum, and relationships among teachers and students and community. It is apparent in every lesson, curriculum guide, unit bulletin board, and letter that is sent home; it can be seen in the process by which books and audiovisual aids are acquired for the library, in the games played during recess, and in the lunch that is served. *Multicultural education is a philosophy, a way of looking at the world, not simply a program or a class or a teacher.*

What might such a pervasive multicultural approach look like in practice? Although a comprehensive approach might vary significantly from school to school, there are a number of general changes that we should expect to see in most institutions. First, the curriculum would have to be completely overhauled to include the perspectives, contributions, and histories of different cultures, races, genders, and classes — not just those of the people in power. Topics that have been traditionally considered controversial and even dangerous, such as racism in the United States, would be discussed in classes and students would be encouraged to reflect on them in order to come to their own conclusions. We would also expect to see a major shift in the way that subject matter is taught in schools to incorporate a variety of instructional strategies so that students from diverse backgrounds and cultures could learn up to their true potential. Teachers would no longer rely on one instructional approach and would become proficient in a number of strategies and techniques that address the needs of different students.

A pervasive multicultural approach would also necessitate the reorganization of public schools as we know them today. This means that schools could no longer be one of the most segregated places in our nation and that drastic changes would be made to integrate the student population so that children from diverse classes and ethnic backgrounds would learn together in the same schools and classes. Efforts would also be made to change the entire school staff so that it is more representative of our country's diversity. Moreover, a reorganization of schools would mean that practices, like tracking, that favor some students over others, be discontinued. Parents and other community members would be invited to collaborate with teachers and staff to design curricula and plan school events. In this way, schools would become learning environments "in which curriculum, pedagogy, and outreach are all consistent with a broadly conceptualized multicultural philosophy" (Nieto 2000, 313).

·CONCLUSION

This chapter has attempted to dispel the widespread myth that multicultural education is essentially about the acknowledgment and appreciation of the heroes, holidays, and traditions of different cultures, nationalities, and religions. Such a notion of multicultural education is inadequate not only because it is far too narrow but also because it fails to acknowledge the institutional racism and discrimination that exist in this country. At the core of multicultural education is the recognition that the United States was founded on the basis of an unjust system of power, one which continues to flourish today, and that the role of education is to help students become more aware of and challenge this system.

To achieve this end, multicultural education must be fundamentally antiracist, as Nieto teaches us, striving to combat the various forms of discrimination and inequality that benefit some students and hurt others. Besides being antiracist, a comprehensive multicultural approach must receive the same weight as other core subjects and be pervasive throughout the school curriculum, climate, and culture. This means that multicultural education should not be reduced to a particular class period that is taught by a specialist and distinct from all other school knowledge. In addition, a broadly conceived multicultural approach has the advantage of helping us avoid the tendency of equating multicultural education with mere content integration. It enables us to realize that multicultural education is just as much about *how* we teach and interact with students as it is about *what* we teach them.

NOTE

1. From a song titled "1492" by Nancy Schimmel. In Bill Bigelow and Bob Peterson, eds. (1998).

Chapter Ten

Easy Solutions Work in Education

I love metaphors. I love metaphors because they provide us with a new way of looking at the world, a fresh perspective from which to analyze the most important problems that perplex us. Metaphors are not definitions, which tell us exactly what a thing is or what a word means. Definitions set limits and boundaries and put restrictions on what we can say or think. Metaphors, on the other hand, are symbols that tell us what something is "like" or analogous to. They refer to things that are representative or suggestive of other things and are therefore less restricting and more open to different interpretations than definitions. So I would like to open the last chapter of this book with a metaphor, a metaphor that points to a new way of looking at the state of education in the United States today.

In Robert Pirsig's classic work from the 1970's *Zen and the Art of Motorcycle Maintenance,* Pirsig, a technical writer, explains to a friend who got stuck trying to assemble an outdoor barbecue rotisserie because the instructions were hard to follow, how instructions like these are put together.

> You go out on the assembly line with a tape recorder and the foreman sends you to talk to the guy he needs least, the biggest goof-off he's got, and whatever he tells you — that's the instructions. The next guy might have told you something completely different and probably better, but he's too busy. (Pirsig 1975, 147)

Pirsig then goes on to explain that what many of us find so frustrating about instructions like these is that they imply that there is only one way to put the rotisserie together — their way. "Actually there are hundreds of ways to put the rotisserie together and when they make you follow just one way without showing you the overall problem the instructions become hard to follow in such a way as not to make mistakes" (Pirsig 1975, 147). Pirsig's point is that the assumption that there is only one way to assemble the rotisserie or any other machine eliminates all the creativity, enthusiasm, and initiative from the construction process. Moreover, as in the case of the rotisserie, the prescribed way of assembling the machine is not likely to be the best way since it was created by the biggest goof-off in the company.

What is the significance of this metaphor for the issue of the state of education in the United States? Keeping in mind the fact that metaphors are not definitions and, therefore, can only tell us what something is like, I would like to propose the following hypothesis: Much of what is wrong with the American education system in the last two decades can be attributed to the fact that many policymakers and educational leaders have assumed that there is only one way to educate our children. On the basis of this assumption, they have created a set of educational standards and procedures that all states, districts, schools, and teachers must follow. If states, districts, and schools choose not to follow these standards, they risk losing federal funding or being hit with other serious sanctions.

The problem is that the standardization of American education and the fact that teachers are required to follow the prescriptions of others rather than think on their own — all lead to a situation in which teachers' creativity, enthusiasm, and initiative are being undermined. Equally problematic is the fact that the standards that teachers are held accountable to are often designed by policymakers and so-called experts with limited classroom experience, knowledge of how students learn, or familiarity with the complexity of schools. As a result, it is very likely that the standards being imposed on schools and teachers are not the best ones to enhance the education of our students. In fact, in many cases these standards and procedures are doing more harm than good. In what follows, I will try to verify this hypothesis by analyzing two major policy initiatives: No Child Left Behind (NCLB) and federal initiatives to deregulate teacher education.

STANDARDIZATION, ACCOUNTABILITY, AND NO CHILD LEFT BEHIND

The 2001 No Child Left Behind Act is considered by many educators as the most far reaching expansion of federal power over the nation's education system in history. According to Richard Elmore (2002, 2),

> the federal government is mandating a single test-based accountability system for all states — a system currently operating in fewer than half the states. The federal government is requiring annual testing at every grade level, and requiring states to disaggregate their test scores by racial and socioeconomic backgrounds — a system currently operating in only a handful of states and one that is fraught with technical difficulties. The federal government is mandating a single definition of adequate yearly progress, the amount by which schools must increase their test scores in order to avoid some sort of sanction — an issue that in the past has been decided jointly by states and the federal government.

Elmore also points out that the federal government has set a single target date by which all students must exceed a state-defined proficiency level, an issue that in the past has been left to the discretion of individual states and school districts.

Historically speaking, prior to the enactment of NCLB, it was essentially up to individual school districts and states to establish academic standards for students and ensure that they were meeting these standards. However, the trend to give the federal government more control accelerated in the mid 1990s when Title I, the national compensatory education program, was amended to require states to create performance-based accountability systems for schools in exchange for receiving federal funding. These new provisions obliged states to "develop academic standards, assessments based on the standards, and progress goals for schools and school districts, all within ambitious timetables" (Elmore 2002, 3). By the year 2000, even though almost all states had developed an assessment program and a way to publicize the results, fewer than half the states had met the federal requirements. That is, most states had failed to make good on their commitment to raise students' performance on standardized tests to a particular level.

Rather than approach this situation as a very complex problem that has social, economic, and political ramifications, the Federal Government opted for an easy solution: tightening the existing law's requirements. And rather than investigating the underlying reasons that more than half of the states were unable to comply with the requirements of Title I, the Administration elected to push for a much more stringent and demanding law. Specifically, in mandating a single test-based accountability system for all states, the federal government is assuming not only that there is only one legitimate way to assess students but also that the standards that we hold students accountable for should be uniform, irrespective of clear differences among students with diverse backgrounds, interests, and abilities. Bearing in mind Pirsig's metaphor, the problem results from two assumptions: that there is just one way to define rigorous academic standards and that national high-stakes tests are the only legitimate instruments that can be used to hold students accountable for these standards.

Let's examine each of these assertions to see if they hold up to close scrutiny. First, let us look at the assumption that there is but one way to define rigorous academic standards. In Chapter Eight I demonstrated that the issue of high or rigorous standards is a complex one and that the supposition that these standards can be equated with the expression of certain facts and skills in a testing situation is simplistic at best. Following the lead of Sizer and others, I tried to show that rigorous academic standards have much more to do with the development of intellectual habits of mind than with the acquisition of a set of basic facts and skills. Still, how one defines high standards will depend on what one perceives is the fundamental purpose of education. Thus, if one thinks that students should graduate from high school with the ability to become productive members of society, then perhaps it is enough to require them to master a set of basic skills and important knowledge. However, if one believes that students should finish schools with the capacity and willingness to become critical and active citizens in a democracy, then it is clear that we should hold them to much higher intellectual standards.

The assumption that there is only one definition of high standards goes hand in hand with the false notion that there is a single right way to teach students the desired skills and knowledge. For instance, the proponents of the federal Reading First mandates of the No Child Left Behind Act have made the presumptuous claim that 90 to 95% of poor readers can be reading on grade level if provided with appropriate instruction. Yet, according to Richard Allington (2004, 25),

> no research suggests that classroom teachers can help 90 to 95 percent of students acquire grade-level reading proficiencies by learning more about phonology, using a scripted curriculum, teaching systematic phonics, or following some "proven" program.

Instead, the research indicates that even the programs that most reliably helped struggling readers, like intensive tutoring provided by experts, raised the achievement of only about half of the poor readers to average levels.

Moreover, we have already known for several years that highly qualified teachers can make a big difference in improving students' learning and in closing the achievement gap between white and minority students. Linda Darling-Hammond, who has studied this issue for years, concluded in a major report (1999) that teacher quality accounted for 40 to 60% of the variance in achievement for fourth and eighth grade reading and math. Similarly, a study conducted in Texas by Ferguson (1991) found that "the large disparities between black and white students were almost entirely accounted for by differences in the qualifications of their teachers." In light of this evidence, it is disturbing that federal initiatives to improve literacy instruction are calling for the use of one method of teaching students how to read as the savior for our national literacy problems. Instead of investing heavily in improving the quality of teachers by increasing their salaries and reducing class size, the supporters of these initiatives are grasping for a simple solution to a very complex problem.

In view of Pirsig's metaphor, it seems pretty obvious that the efforts to impose a single method of reading instruction are likely to undermine teachers' enthusiasm and initiative for designing and conducting creative lessons. Since teachers are now being required to merely implement a particular literacy program that was created by others, they are not likely to become as skillful as those who are given a problem and the freedom to design and apply different solutions to address this problem. In addition, while the method of reading instruction that is being imposed on teachers may work well for some students, it is not likely, as the research suggests, to succeed with *all* students. Thus we are shortchanging many students, particularly the ones who struggle the most, when we pretend that we can get good results by simply teaching everybody in the same way. Such an assumption flies in the face of what we have known for years — that since children differ in terms of their interests, abilities, and backgrounds, good teachers are ones who vary their instruction to accommodate these differences.

The second assumption that needs to be examined is that annual high-stakes assessments are the only instruments that can hold schools, teachers, and students accountable for the standards that have been set. This assertion is problematic because most of the high-stakes tests are seriously flawed in that they contain numerous items that were never taught, exclude items that teachers have emphasized, and measure other factors besides the quality of instruction such as students' inherited academic aptitude. Most of the standardized tests that are used today simply cannot provide us with accurate data about the quality of schooling. Furthermore, as shown in Chapter Eight, the testing movement has led to the narrowing of the curriculum and to reliance on a pedagogy based on drill and memorization.

If standardized achievement tests cannot accurately measure the quality of schooling, then we should consider other ways of evaluating students that are more reliable at assessing students' actual learning and performance. I am referring to performance tasks such as portfolios of students' work, teachers' evaluations of their students, student-initiated projects, and formal exhibitions of students' work. Research indicates that these performance tasks are better measures of students' learning because they are more challenging than standardized tests and require students to understand the material well enough to explain it to others (Sizer 1996, 84). Unlike standardized exams that measure what students remember at a particular moment, performance-based assessments focus on what students have actually learned and are able to do over a period of time.

So why do policymakers and educational leaders continue to push for standardized tests as the main instrument to measure student achievement when the evidence suggests that these assessments are so flawed? The answer is not altogether surprising: These tests are relatively inexpensive to administer; they do not require much time to implement; and they deliver clear, visible results (Elmore 2002, 2). Yet, the apparent "advantages" of standardized tests are not nearly enough to justify the numerous educational shortcomings that these instruments entail, such as a narrowing of the curriculum and a growing emphasis on teaching to the test.

What's more, a serious problem arises when we use "test scores to make decisions about students academic progress — decisions about whether they can advance to the next grade or graduate from high school" (Elmore 2002, 7). The problem is that it is both ethically and empirically wrong to make consequential decisions about individual students, ones that could impact their life chances, based on a test score. Ethically, it is not right to limit people's possibilities in life, like their chance of going to college or getting a good job, especially for those that did not have the same advantages as others. And empirically speaking, the fact is that test scores have a significant margin of error associated with them, thus making it very difficult to know if an individual score is reliable or not.

Keeping Pirsig's rotisserie instructions metaphor in mind, it is becoming increasingly obvious that the people behind NCLB and the standardization of education know very little about the complex realities of schools and about what it would take to drastically improve the education of our children. In Elmore's (2002, 2) words:

> If this shift in federal policy were based on the accumulated wisdom gained from experiences with accountability in states, districts, and schools, or if it were based on clear design principles that had some basis in practice, it might be worth the risk. In fact, however, this shift is based on little more than policy talk among people who know hardly anything about the institutional realities of accountability and even less about the problems of improving instruction in schools.

THE DEREGULATION OF TEACHER EDUCATION

Another major policy initiative that is under debate in the past few years is the effort to deregulate teacher education. In his 2002 Annual Report on Teacher Quality (*Meeting the Highly Qualified Teacher Challenge*), former Secretary of Education Rod Paige argues for "the dismantling of teacher education systems and the redefinition of teacher qualifications to include little preparation for teaching" (Darling-Hammond and Youngs 2002, 13). Basing its argument on the assumption that teacher education is not related to teacher effectiveness, the report calls for the redefinition of certification to emphasize higher standards of verbal ability and content knowledge at the expense of pedagogical knowledge and practice. The report also advocates alternative certification programs that make it much easier for individuals to become teachers without providing them with much educational background or preparation for teaching.

To support its recommendations, the Secretary's report (2002, 19) claims that "there is little evidence that education school course work leads to improved student achievement," but offers very little scientific research to support this claim. One of the few studies that the Secretary's report cites as proof of its assertion about the lack of connection between teacher education and certification and student achievement is a report by Kate Walsh from 2001 titled *Teacher Certification Reconsidered: Stumbling for Quality*. However, Linda Darling-Hammond and Peter Youngs (2002, 13-14), who closely examined Walsh's report, argue that it "excludes much of the evidence on the topic, misrepresents many research findings, makes inaccurate claims about studies that have examined the consequences of preparation, and uses a double standard in evaluating the research." Hence, the fact that the Secretary's report rests on the shaky conclusions of a flawed study rather than on rigorous scientific research or deep philosophical thinking is enough to make us question its credibility.

In fact, a variety of studies using national, state, and local data have come to the exact opposite conclusion: there is *a significant relationship between teacher education and certification measures and student performance* (Goldhaber and Brewer 2000; Betts, Reuben, and Danenberg 2000; and Darling-Hammond 2000). Darling-Hammond and Youngs, who examined these different studies, assert that there are a number of aspects of teacher qualifications that have an impact on student achievement. Besides verbal ability and the content knowledge that Paige's report acknowledges as being significant, other factors such as knowledge about teaching and learning as reflected in teacher education courses, as well as teaching experience were also found to have a positive impact on student achievement. The fact that this report recognizes only the former variables and not the latter should leave us wondering if his concern is actually to enhance teacher quality. Perhaps he is really interested in deregulating teacher education in order to open the door for alternative certification programs that will help address the teacher shortage problem.

To be sure, one could make the argument that the deregulation of teacher education is meant to combat a genuine problem in this country, the growing shortage of quality teachers. According to Hoffman (2004, 121), the qualified teacher shortage will have the greatest impact on schools serving children of poverty, and the number of individuals willing to commit to teaching in inner-city settings serving minority students is dwindling at the same time as these student populations are growing. In Chicago, journalists in an award-winning investigative report found that 55% of the teachers at one Chicago inner-city school were not fully certified to teach their students. They went on to report that one in five teachers in Chicago's most needy schools was unqualified to teach (Grossman, Beaupre, and Rossi 2001). Similar research found that less than half of the teachers in some New York City's schools held certification in the subject area they taught. This study concluded that low-income, low-achieving, and non-white students were more likely to have teachers who lacked prior teaching experience, had failed a teacher-licensing exam on the first try, or had attended less selective colleges as undergraduates (Olson 2003, 10).

Still, there is little evidence to support the claim that we can solve the qualified teacher shortage by deregulating teacher education and implementing nationwide alternative certification programs that streamline the certification process and make it easier for talented individuals to become teachers. As Marilyn Cochran-Smith (2004, 5) writes,

> it is simply not the case, for example, that there is a robust body of evidence indicating that we can solve the problem of teacher supply simultaneously with the problem of teacher quality by implementing statewide or nationwide alternate routes into teaching. As a matter of fact, syntheses of the empirical research on alternate routes indicate that the evidence is skimpy and inconclusive, making policy recommendations nearly impossible.

What is much more likely to happen, according to Cochran-Smith, with the proliferation of alternate certification programs is the creation "of a two-tiered educational system wherein the pupils most in need of fully qualified and fully licensed teachers are the least likely to get them." Evidence of this two-tiered system is beginning to emerge. For instance, New York City has recently launched a program called the *NYC Teaching Fellows*, a program designed to recruit talented professionals to teach in some of the city's most underperforming schools. The Fellows, who for the most part have little formal background in education and no classroom experience, receive a crash course in various aspects of education and are then assigned to teach in disadvantaged schools primarily in the Bronx and Brooklyn. Obviously, these inexperienced and untested teachers would never be hired to teach in the wealthy suburbs or in other advantaged neighborhoods of New York City. So whereas alternative certification programs like the *NYC Teaching Fellows* may be helping states alleviate the immediate problem of teacher supply, they do not really do much to address the issue of the lack of qualified teachers for poor and other disadvantaged children. Indeed, such programs are likely to perpetuate the qualified teacher gap between wealthy and poor school districts by assigning ill prepared teachers to teach in some of the most struggling schools.

In light of Pirsig's rotisserie instruction metaphor, what is striking about the current initiatives to deregulate teacher education is that these efforts are simply incoherent and do not make sense. For example, Cochran-Smith (2004, 4) calls our attention to the fact that the Department of Education's initiative to deregulate teacher education is ironically coupled with intensified regulation: "At the federal level (and in some states), deregulation and regulation have become strange but intimate bedfellows, advocating seemingly contradictory but simultaneous efforts to deregulate *and* tightly regulate teacher preparation" (Cochran-Smith 2004, 4). On the one hand, DOE reports point to the need to have tighter federal control of teacher preparation in that they analyze the results of mandatory annual state report on the quality of teacher preparation programs. Yet, on the other hand, the reports explicitly favor deregulation, especially in the form of alternative certification programs that seriously undermine the role of colleges and universities in teacher preparation. Of course, Paige's report does not bother to explain how these seemingly contradictory policies can coexist with each other.

In effect, his assertion that the qualified teacher shortage can be alleviated by deregulating teacher education simply does not hold up. What is much more likely to happen is that the deregulation of teacher education will result in the certification of teachers who do not have the necessary preparation or skills that enable them to successfully promote student learning. For instance, a study conducted with 136 principals and more than 200 teachers in New Hampshire found that alternate route teachers were rated by their principals significantly lower on instructional skills and planning than traditionally certified teachers. The traditionally certified teachers in this study rated their own preparation significantly higher than did those certified in alternate routes (Darling-Hammond and Youngs 2002, 23). While it is true that alternative certification programs vary significantly from each other and that some programs are better than others, it is also true that the majority of them "feature very short initial training followed by immediate classroom responsibility with concurrent on-the-job and course training" (Cochran-Smith 2004, 5). For this reason, it is not surprising that many of the new teachers who graduate from an alternative certification program are unprepared to teach. Obviously, the American public would never stand for a federal policy that promoted the quick preparation and placement of other professionals like doctors and lawyers.

Moreover, according to Cochran-Smith (2004, 5), there is a possibility that the coupling of deregulation with increased regulation of teacher education will result in a situation in which we get the worst of both worlds:

> wholesale support for alternate routes that do away with most teacher requirements and make entry into teaching wide open, on one hand, and centralized control that diminishes state- and local-level decisions about the preparation of teachers and greatly prescribes professional discretion and autonomy, on the other.

If this prediction holds up, the deregulation of teacher education may very well lead to the certification of more teachers who are mediocre or unqualified to teach in the public schools. Similarly, the increase of federal regulation of teacher preparation will likely result in a situation in which more teachers are alienated from their work because they are forced to spend most of their time trying to follow the prescriptions of others.

Ultimately, I suspect that federal initiatives to alleviate the qualified teacher shortage will fail because they promote the proliferation of teacher preparation programs that are weak and incoherent. Much like the disjointed instructions to assemble the rotisserie in Pirsig's metaphor, these programs will produce teachers who are confused about the general purpose of education in a democratic society. Perhaps these teachers will be skilled at preparing their students to take the standardized tests, but they will most likely lack an awareness of the genuine meaning of teaching and learning. My intent here is not to advocate more regulation of teacher education, but to suggest that there is great danger in assuming that the qualified teacher shortage is a simple problem that can be addressed by implementing a quick and easy solution. As Rice (2003, vii) argues,

the evidence indicates that neither an extreme centralized bu-
reaucratization nor a complete deregulation of teacher requirements is a wise approach for improving teacher
quality.... Education policymakers and administrators
would be well served by recognizing the complexity of the issue and adopting multiple measures along many dimensions
to support existing teachers and to attract and hire new,
highly qualified teachers.

RECLAIMING THE LEGACY OF SOCRATES

Anyone familiar with the legacy of Socrates as it appears in the dialogues of Plato knows that he loved to engage in dialogues with his fellow
citizens from Athens. Socrates was relentless in his search for the truth. He
was an expert at examining the opinions of his dialogue partners and evaluating them from multiple perspectives to see if they hold up to the test of
reason and experience. Perhaps this is one of the reasons that the dialogues that Socrates takes part in so often seem to go around in circles, analyzing the same problem from different points of view, but never really
reaching a definitive answer. Yet while it is true that Socrates does not provide us with conclusive definitions of virtue, justice, or love, he does help
us gain a better understanding of these very complex and rich concepts.
As such, Socrates embodies what it means to be a critical thinker: a person
who takes nothing for granted and continuously engages in the process of
questioning, doubting, analyzing, and revising his ideas.

So what can we learn from the legacy of Socrates about how we
should assess the two educational policies discussed in this chapter?
Generally speaking, my analysis suggests that both the accountability
policy that is included in the No Child Left Behind Act and the federal
initiatives to deregulate teacher education are not based on the kind of
deep philosophical thinking that Socrates engaged in. On the contrary,
these federal policies rest on a hollow and baseless agenda of a number
of educational leaders who seem to be more interested in finding quick
fixes to complex educational problems than in understanding the underlying causes of these problems. To think, for example, that we can simply
alleviate the achievement gap between white, middle class and minority,
lower class students by mandating a single test-based accountability
system makes no sense because this remedy disregards the reasons that
the struggling students were failing the previous tests and the kind of
support they need to succeed in schools. Indeed, one of the main cri-

tiques of the NCLB by educators across the country has been that the administration has mandated a host of new requirements that teachers, schools, and states must meet without adequately supporting and funding the new mandates (Mathis 2003).

Besides the fact that the new federal policies discussed here are not based on a deep philosophical analysis, my study indicates that these policies are not supported by scientifically based research or by the experience of teachers. For one, there is virtually no evidence to support the claim that annual, high-stakes testing is the only, or even best, way to hold schools, teachers, and students accountable for the new standards. Sizer's extensive experience with the Coalition of Essential Schools confirms the view that Exhibitions and other performance-based tasks rather than standardized tests are assessment tools that really challenge students and hold them accountable for rigorous standards. And Joe Kincheloe's research (2001) on standards of complexity demonstrates that the standards that we should require of future citizens in a democratic society are not assessed by the current high-stakes exams.

Finally, the policy recommendations to address the qualified teacher shortage by deregulating teacher education and streamlining the certification process are not backed up by the available evidence. Instead, most of the studies reviewed here as well as my own experience indicate that teachers who graduate from traditional teacher education programs are better prepared and more knowledgeable than ones who went through alternative certification programs. In fact, these studies show that teacher preparation — including education course work and student teaching — contribute at least as much as verbal ability and content knowledge to outcomes such as teacher effectiveness and teacher retention (Darling-Hammond and Youngs 2002, 23). Common sense tells us that to cultivate qualified teachers we need to provide teacher candidates with the kind of experiences that will prepare them for the challenges they will encounter in the public schools. Testing candidates on their verbal ability and instructing them in content knowledge is not nearly enough to prepare them to become qualified teachers.

References

Apple Computer, Inc. 2002 Fall/2003 Spring. The impact of technology on student achievement: A summary of research findings on technology's impact in the classroom. *Canadian Technology and Business*, pp. 41-44.

Apple, Michael W. 1979. *Ideology and curriculum*. Boston: Routledge.

Apple, Michael W. 1996. *Cultural politics and education*. New York: Teachers College Press.

Apple, Michael W. 2000. *Official knowledge: Democratic education in a conservative age*. New York: Routledge.

Apple, Michael W. 2001, May/June. Markets, standards, teaching, and teacher education. *Journal of Teacher Education* 52(3).

Allington, R. L. 2004. Setting the record straight. *Educational Leadership* 61(6): 22-25.

Armstrong, Alison, and Charles Casement. 2000. *The child and the machine: Why computers may put our children's education at risk*. Beltsville, MD: Robins Lane Press.

Ayers, W. 1995. *To become a teacher: Making a difference in children's lives*. New York: Teachers College Press.

Baldwin, James. 1963, December 21. A talk to teachers. *Saturday Review*.

Banks, James. 1996. *Multicultural education: Historical and contemporary perspectives*. New York: Teachers College Press.

Banks, James, and Cherry A. McGee Banks. 1997. *Multicultural education: Issues and perspectives*, 3rd ed. Boston: Allyn and Bacon.

Bekham-Hungler, D., C. Williams, K. Smith, and C. Dudley-Marling. 2003. Teaching words that students misspell: Spelling instruction and young children's writing. *Language Arts* 80(4).

Betts, J. R., K. S. Rueben, and A. Danenberg. 2000. *Equal resources, equal outcomes? The distribution of school resources and student achievement in California*. San Francisco: Public Policy Institute of California.

Bigelow, Bill, and Bob Peterson. 1998. *Rethinking Columbus: The next 500 years*. Milwaukee: Rethinking Schools.

Brell, David. 2001. Teaching as moral enterprise. *Encounter: Education for Meaning and Social Justice* 14(2): 23-29.

Brophy, Jere. 1986. Teacher influences on student achievement. *American Psychologist* 41(10).

Bryson, M., and S. de Castel. 1998. New technologies and the cultural ecology of primary schooling: Imagining teachers as Luddites in/deed. *Educational Policy* 12: 542-567.

Buber, M. 1955. The education of character. In *Between man and man,* translated by Ronald Gregor Smith. Boston: Beacon Press.

Canter, L., and M. Canter. 1992. *Lee Canter's Assertive Discipline: Positive behavior management for today's classroom.* Santa Monica, CA: Canter & Associates.

Casas, Mary. 2003. The use of standardized tests in assessing authentic learning: A contradiction indeed. *Teachers College Record* online journal.

Cochran-Smith, M. 2004. Taking stock in 2004: Teacher education in dangerous times. *Journal of Teacher Education* 55(1).

Cooper, Eric J. 1989. Toward a new mainstream of instruction for American schools. *Journal of Negro Education* 58(1).

Cuban, Larry. 2001. *Oversold & underused: Computers in the classroom.* Cambridge, MA: Harvard University Press.

Darling-Hammond, L. 1999. *Doing what matters most: Investing in quality teaching.* New York: National Commission on Teaching and America's Future.

Darling-Hammond, L. 2000. Teacher quality and student achievement: A review of state policy evidence. *Education Policy Analysis Archives* 8(1).

Darling-Hammond, L., and P. Youngs. 2002. Defining "highly qualified teachers": What does "scientifically-based research" actually tell us? *Educational Researcher* 31(9).

Deal, Terrence E., and Kent D. Peterson. 1999. *Shaping school culture: The heart of leadership.* San Francisco: Jossey-Bass.

Dewey, John. 1956. The school and society. In *The child and the curriculum, the school and society.* Chicago: University of Chicago Press.

Dewey, John. 1966. *Democracy and education.* New York: Free Press.

Dwyer, D. C. 1996. The imperative to change our schools. In *Education and technology: Reflections on computing in classrooms,* edited by C. Fisher, D. Dwyer, and K. Yocam. San Francisco: Jossey-Bass.

Elmore, R. 2002, Spring. Unwarranted intrusion. *Education next.*

Evertson, Carolyn M., Edmund T. Emmer, and Murray E. Worsham. 2000. *Classroom management for elementary teachers.* Boston: Allyn and Bacon.

Ferguson, R. F. 1991. Paying for public education: New evidence on how and why money matters. *Harvard Journal on Legislation* 28: 465-491.

Fielding, R. 2003, January 15. IT in schools fails to raise standards. London: VNU Business Publications.

Freiberg, Jerome H. 1999. *Beyond Behaviorism: Changing the classroom management paradigm.* Needham Heights, MA: Allyn and Bacon.

Freire, P. 1994. *Pedagogy of the oppressed.* Translated by Myra Bergman Ramos. New York: Continuum.

Gatto, John Taylor. 2002. *Dumbing us down: The hidden curriculum of compulsory schooling.* Gabriola Island, BC: New Society.

Goldhaber, D. D., and D. J. Brewer. 2000. Does teacher certification matter? High school teacher certification status and student achievement. *Education Evaluation and Policy Analysis* 22(2): 129-146.

Good, Thomas L., and Jere E. Brophy. 2000. *Looking in classrooms,* 8th ed. New York: Longman.

Gordon, Mordechai. 2003. Standards, testing, and educational reform: The politics of false generosity." *Encounter: Education for Meaning and Social Justice* 16(2).

Greene, Maxine. 2000. The ambiguities of freedom. *English Education* 33(1).

Grossman, K. N., B. Beaupre, and R. Rossi. 2001, September 7. Poorest kids often wind up with the weakest teachers. *Chicago Sun Times.*

Grumet. 1995. The curriculum: What are the basics and why are we teaching them? In *Thirteen questions: Reframing Education's Conversation,* edited by Kincheloe and Steinberg. New York: Peter Lang.

Hoffman, J. V. 2004. Achieving the goal of a quality teacher of reading for every classroom: Divest, test or invest? *Reading Research Quarterly* 39(1): 119-128.

hooks, bell. 1994. *Teaching to transgress: Education as the practice of freedom.* New York: Routledge.

Jackson, Philip W., Robert E. Boostrom, and David T. Hansen. 1993. *The moral life of schools.* San Francisco: Jossey-Bass.

Jambor, Tom. 1994. School recess and social development. *Dimensions of Early Childhood* 23(1).

Kane, J. 1998, Spring. The new language of reform. *Encounter: Education for Meaning and Social Justice* 11(1): 2-3.

Kincheloe, Joe. 2001. Hope in the shadows: Reconstructing the debate over educational standards. In *Standards and schooling in the United*

States: An encyclopedia, edited by Joe L. Kincheloe and Danny Weil. Santa Barbara, CA: ABC-CLIO.

Kincheloe, J. L., and S. R. Steinberg. 1995. *Thirteen questions: Reframing education's conversation*. New York: Peter Lang.

Kincheloe, J. L., S. R. Steinberg, and L. E. Villaverde. 1999. *Rethinking intelligence: Confronting psychological assumptions about teaching and learning*. New York: Routledge.

Kobrin, David. 1995. Let the future write the past: Classroom collaboration, primary sources, and the making of high schools historians. *The History Teacher* 28(4).

Kohn, Alfie. 1996. *Beyond discipline: From compliance to community*. Alexandria, VA: ASCD.

Kozol, Jonathan. 1992. *Savage inequalities: Children in America's schools*. New York: Harper Perennial.

Lewis, Anne. 2002, November. A horse called NCLB. *Phi Delta Kappan* 84(3).

Loewen, James W. 1996. *Lies my teacher told me: Everything your American history textbook got wrong*. New York: Touchstone.

Loughran, John, and Jeff Northfield. 1996. *Opening the classroom door: Teacher researcher learner*. Bristol, PA: Falmer Press.

Mathis, W. J. 2003. No Child Left Behind: Costs and benefits. *Phi Delta Kappan* 84(9).

McKeon, Richard. 1947. *Introduction to Aristotle*, edited by Richard McKeon. New York: Modern Library.

Michie, G. 1999. *Holler if you hear me: The education of a teacher and his students*. New York: Teachers College Press.

Miller, Ron. 1997. *What are schools for? Holistic education in American culture*. Brandon, VT: Holistic Education Press.

Nieto, Sonia. 2000. *Affirming diversity: The sociopolitical context of multicultural education*, 3rd ed. New York: Longman.

Olson, L. 2003. January 9. The great divide. *Education Week* 18: 9-16.

Ozmon, Howard A., and Samuel M. Craver. 1999. *Philosophical foundations of education*, 6th ed. Upper Saddle River, NJ: Merrill.

Paige, Rod. 2004, February 27. Focus on the children. Op-Ed article in *The Washington Post*.

Pellegrini, A. D. 1991. Outdoor recess: Is it really necessary? *Principal* 70(5).

Pellegrini, A. D., and C. D. Glickman. 1989. The educational role of recess. *Principal* 62(5).

Persell, C. H. 1977. *Education and inequality: A theoretical and empirical synthesis*. New York: Free Press.

Pirsig, Robert M. 1974. *Zen and the art of motorcycle maintenance*. New York: Bantam.

Popham, W. James 2001. *The truth about testing: An educator's call to action*. Alexandria, VA: ASCD.

Postman, Neil. 1997. Science and the story we need. *First Things* 69: 29-32.

Rice, J. K. 2003. *Teacher quality: Understanding the effectiveness of teacher attributes*. Washington, DC: Economic Policy Institute.

Robertson, Heather-Jane. 2003. Toward a theory of negativity: Teacher education and information and communications technology. *Journal of Teacher Education* 54(4).

Rousseau, Jean-Jacques. 1979. *Emile or On Education*. Translated by Allan Bloom. New York: Basic Books.

Russell, Michael, Damien Bebell, Laura O'Dwyer, and Kathleen O'Connor. 2003. Examining teacher technology use: Implications for preservice and inservice teacher preparation. *Journal of Teacher Education* 54(4).

Sacks, Peter. 1999 *Standardized minds: The high price of America's testing culture and what we can do to change it*. Cambridge, MA: Perseus.

Schofield, Janet Ward, and Ann Locke Davidson. 2002. *Bringing the Internet to school: Lessons from an urban district*. San Francisco, CA: Jossey-Bass.

Sizer, Theodore R. 1996. *Horace's hope: What works for the American high school*. New York: Houghton Mifflin.

U.S. Department of Education. 2002. *Meeting the highly qualified teacher challenge: The Secretary's annual report on teacher quality*. Washington DC: U.S. Department of Education, Office of Postsecondary Education.

Vygotsky, L. S. 1978. *Mind in society: The development of higher psychological processes*. Cambridge, MA: Harvard University Press.

Walsh, K. 2001. *Teacher certification reconsidered: Stumbling for quality*. Baltimore: Abell Foundation.

Warmington, Eric H., and Philip G. Rouse. 1956. *Great dialogues of Plato*. Translated by W. H. D. Rouse. New York: Mentor.

Zigler, Edward F., and Matia Finn Stevenson. 1993. *Children in a changing world: Development and social issues*. Pacific Grove, CA: Brooks/Cole.

About the Author

Mordechai Gordon

MORDECHAI GORDON, father of two, is an Associate Professor of Education in the Division of Education at Quinnipiac University in Hamden, Connecticut. Professor Gordon's areas of specialization include the foundations of education, teacher education, and democratic education. He is the editor of *Hannah Arendt and Education: Renewing our Common World*, winner of the 2002 AESA Critics Choice Award. He has written numerous articles that have appeared in such scholarly journals as *Educational Theory*, *Journal of Thought*, and *Encounter: Education for Meaning and Social Justice*.